CALIFORNIA

CONTENTS

Published by Thomas Cook Publishing
The Thomas Cook Group Ltd
PO Box 227, Thorpe Wood
Peterborough PE3 6PU
United Kingdom

Telephone: 01733 503571
E–mail: books@thomascook.com

ISBN 1 841570 35 4

Distributed in the United States of America by the Globe Pequot Press,
PO Box 480, Guilford, Connecticut 06437, USA.

Distributed in Canada by Whitecap Books, 351 Lynn Avenue,
North Vancouver, British Columbia, Canada V7J 2C4.

Distributed in Australia and New Zealand by Peribo Pty Limited,
58 Beaumont Road, Mt Kuring-Gai, NSW, 2080, Australia.

Publisher: Stephen York
Commissioning Editor: Deborah Parker
Map Editor: Bernard Horton

Series Editor: Christopher Catling

Written and researched by: Silk Longview and Lloyd Evans

Cover photograph: Maxine Cass

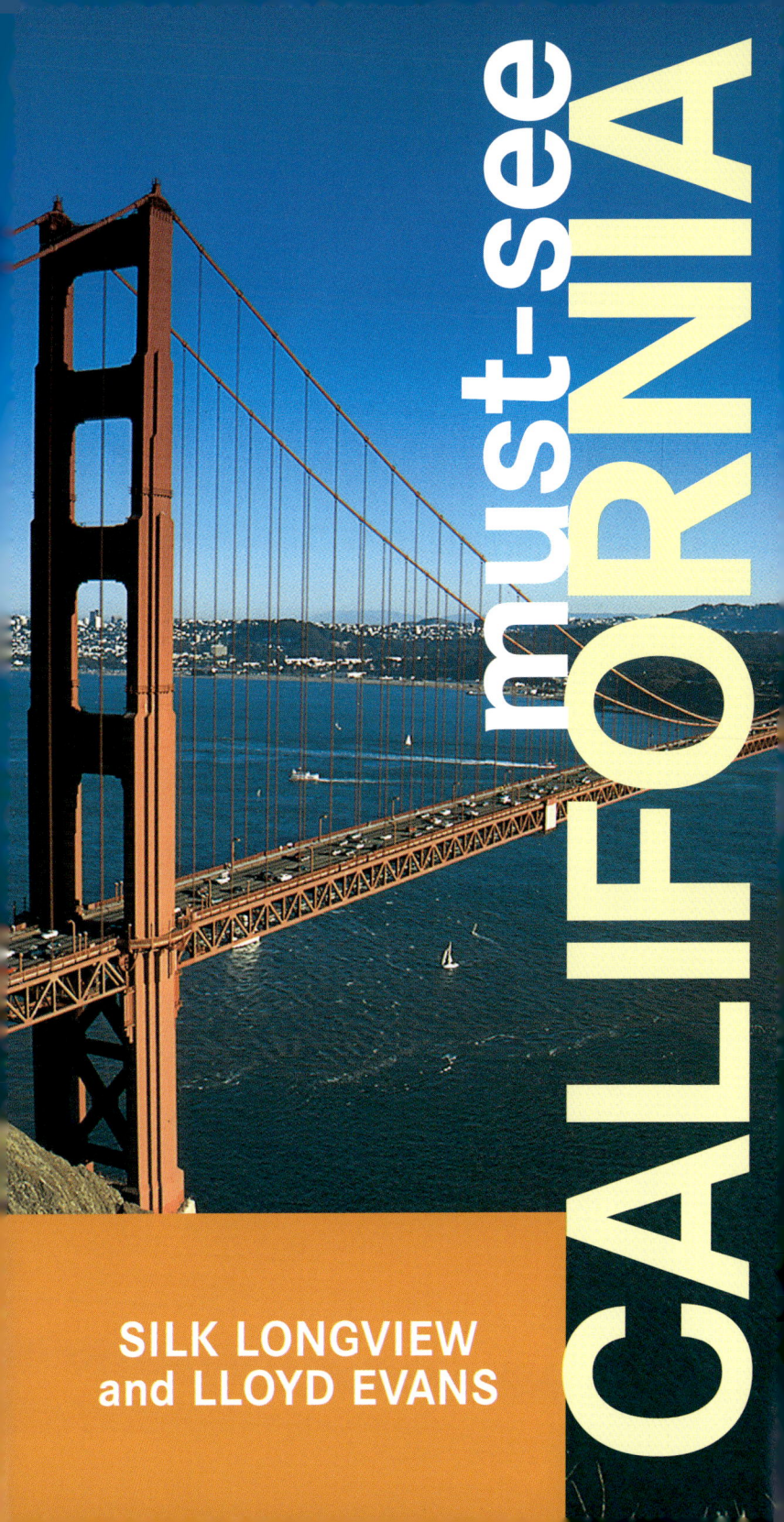

must-see CALIFORNIA

**SILK LONGVIEW
and LLOYD EVANS**

Getting to know California

Discovering California

California is as much a state of mind as a state in America, a place that takes perverse delight in bringing polar opposites into uneasy synthesis. Telephone books list the Church of Satan next to the Church of St John. Iconoclastic jazz saxophonist **John Coltrane** *is canonised while* **transvestite nuns** *in wimples, stiletto heels and five o'clock shadow debate the true meaning of Easter, charity and good works with Roman Catholic Church prelates – and win.*

Named for a novel and developed by dreamers and schemers, California has become a cauldron seething with peoples, places and experiences, from windblown deserts to hip-hop urban landscapes, from manicured vineyard rows, where water is dispensed drop by drop, to vast forests that have yet to be mapped. Newcomers are unthinkingly forgiven for assuming that they've wandered into an asylum where the inmates have taken over. They have, and they have.

Half-myths and half-truths

In the four centuries since Europeans first laid eyes on California, the place has become a land of half-myths, half-truths and outright lies.

California history is more fable than fact, sometimes salutary, sometimes salacious and always open to reinterpretation. Even the few Californians who were born here can't always tell the difference, presuming they would want to. For the most part, nobody bothers.

'Remake Reality' could be the state motto. The state was settled *en masse* by **gold-seekers** who were determined to let nothing stand in the way of fortune, if not fame. And, despite the odds, many of them succeeded, if not in the gold fields, then in the stores, farms and cities that sprang up to supply the mines. Good fortune wasn't universal, but it was enough to feed an irrepressible, irresistible California Dream with equal parts hope, sweat and invention, all saturated with an unflagging optimism that tomorrow *will* be a better day.

The great adventure continues

Pick your preferred reality. Blessed with thousands of square miles of **wilderness**, California claims some of America's most densely populated **urban pockets**. Home to an **international cult of youth and beauty**, it supports the nation's fastest-growing **elderly population**. In a land where *everyone* is descended from **immigrants**, politicians raise an ominous spectre of foreign hordes waiting to flood across the border at every election.

Contradictory? Self-delusional? California wouldn't have it any other way. Californians imagine themselves caught up in a great adventure, a never-ending journey to a land that might be and a state of transcendence that ought to be. Call it a dream, call it arrested adolescence, call it insane, but California is never boring.

A day in the life of California

*It's 0200 and the phone lines are humming. Computers are sucking data from across the globe. On-line surfers are spinning the World Wide Web faster, further and denser. **Telecommuters** are getting real work done after their office-bound co-workers have gone home for the day.*

Welcome to California, where the day slows after midnight, but never stops. In the state that likes to believe that anything can happen, what *has* happened is hard work, hard play and a rush to embrace the future even before tomorrow has quite arrived.

California has never been a place to wait. *Carpe diem*, **seize the day**, might have been invented here, except that nobody has time for dead languages such as Latin or the Queen's English. On buses and schoolyards, it's *Spanglish*, a seamless blend of Spanish and English, and *Chinglish*, Chinese-plus-English, leading a whole alphabet soup of *-glishes*. Computer-speak has wormed into the general consciousness, *beavering* from the techno-serfs who work like beavers building computer codes 60 hours a week, *face time* in those rare moments when face-to-face conversation replaces free-form e-mail, *knowledge base* for the trivia it takes to survive the technological frontier.

Distance, physical distance, is almost irrelevant. In a state that stretches 1200 miles end to end, a 100-mile daily commute – each way – doesn't even rate a raised eyebrow. Driving an hour for dinner is commonplace, even if that hour takes you only 10 miles from home.

Telecommuters have effectively turned California into its own multinational, linking programmers in India with debuggers in Scotland and paper-shufflers in Jamaica. Home-grown high-tech centres have sprung up in every scenic corner of the state. Sierra Nevada hamlets such as **Angels Camp**, **Fish Camp** and **El Portal**, once known for the natural wonders and muscle-straining recreation opportunities near by, have become electronic extensions of **Silicon Valley**. **Marin County**, just north of San Francisco (and 80 per cent protected open space), has blossomed into the third largest multimedia centre on earth in a thoroughly modern meld of computers, artistry and outdoor recreation.

Recreation itself has become big business. California has been one of the world's most popular tourist destinations for decades, and never more popular than among Californians themselves. Physical fitness is a booming religion, exercise its daily sacrament. **Runners**, **cyclists** and **power walkers** are everyday sights in even the most remote towns. **Gymnasiums** and **health clubs** are no longer elite retreats, they're **24-hour-a-day temples** devoted to helping nature undo the ravages that time has wrought. And if exercise isn't enough to restore perfection – or if it's just too much bother – check out the full-page adverts for plastic surgery and age-reducing hormone treatments.

Fanaticism blows on every breeze. If it isn't physical fitness, it's food. Or wine. Or beer. Bread. Water. Baby vegetables. Exotic greens. Free-range poultry. Organic meat. Milk *without* artificial growth hormones. Milk *with* artificial growth hormones. Vintage varieties of apples and vegetables that are nearly extinct and bio-engineered maize that can't even reproduce itself without laboratory help. If it's wired, trendy, cutting-edge, it's California.

Yesterday and tomorrow

California is a story in the making. The very name of the place was borrowed from a 1510 Spanish romantic novel, Las Sergas de Esplandián (The Adventures of Esplandian), *imagined by Garcí Ordóñez de Montalvo as an island peopled by black-skinned Amazons who wielded weapons made of pure gold. Four centuries later, Spanish-speakers are the largest minority in a* **cultural patchwork** *that has been evolving since 1769.*

That's when Spain got around to planting its first colony in California. Europeans had been wandering through California since **Juan Rodriguez Cabrillo** visited San Diego Bay in 1542. Spain, occupied with looting South America of gold, silver, gems and sugar, saw no reason to colonise California, a land without obvious value until England laid claim to British Columbia in 1768.

Spain's response to England's claims on the Pacific coast was a tiny mission and an ill-supplied military garrison at San Diego. The grand plan: a series of **missions**, a day's journey apart, to Hispanicise and Christianise the Native American population and turn California into a self-supporting buffer against English expansion to the south. The reality: a chain of 21 missions stretching from San Diego to Sonoma (north of San Francisco) which imported European diseases that decimated the Indian population, enslaved the survivors and turned California firmly toward the future.

Spain lost California when Mexico claimed independence in 1821; Mexico lost California when three dozen American immigrants seized the abandoned *presidio* or fort, at **Sonoma** in 1846 and declared the **Republic of California**, possibly with covert encouragement from the US government. A month later, the US Navy sailed into Monterey and California became American.

It was a lucky acquisition. **Gold** was discovered less than two years later, sparking a cycle of boom, immigration and boom that has yet to stop. As the gold gave out, silver was discovered, followed by **agriculture, oil**, **manufacturing**, **Hollywood** and **Silicon Valley**. Dreams of success and wealth have lured optimists and schemers from the entire world to California, creating a constantly shifting web of conflict and co-operation held together by an almost religious faith that in California, *anything* is possible.

The land that began as a human patchwork of dozens of small Indian tribes speaking mutually incomprehensible languages has turned full circle. Spain and Mexico shattered California's Native populations; Hispanic California was overrun by waves of mostly American and European immigrants. White California, in turn, has been submerged by successive waves from Asia, Africa, Mexico, Central and South America. The result is an **ethnic and cultural mosaic** with no clear boundaries and no clear majority.

The lines continue to blur. Whites are the largest among dozens of minority groups, with Hispanic and Asian numbers growing rapidly. On the world stage, cultural and economic ties to everywhere have helped California build new markets, attract new innovators and create the **sixth largest economy** on earth. Population and proximity have thrust designers, architects and everyone else into associations and influences that none might have sought out but all have used to advantage. No bets on where the saga will lead, but the long, strange trip that is California continues.

People and places

The **cult of personality** has come to full flower in California. Fame (and fortune) aren't measured in dollars, but in name. Specifically, how many names. The merely famous find it necessary to use two names, ie Steve Martin (cinema); Wolfgang Puck (chef); Larry Ellison (computers). The transcendent have left surnames behind to soar into the public gaze by first name only: Robin (Williams, film and comedy); Jeremiah (Tower, chef); Steve (Jobs, computers). If you have to ask which Robin, Jeremiah or Steve in conversation, you don't deserve to know.

The first-name-only affectation is hardly unique to California, but if the state were a disease, the World Health Organisation would long ago have declared a pandemic and instituted strict quarantine measures.

Too late. From highbrow to no brow, California has taken root in every corner of the world. Cultural preservationists from Canada to Iran have tried to uproot its seedlings, but the sheer force of personality, fame and financial success has given California cultural clout far beyond its mere size.

- The most-watched television programme on earth: the Academy of Motion Picture Arts and Sciences' annual Oscar awards.
- The cinema capital of the world: Hollywood.

- The most popular headquarters city for music recording labels: Los Angeles.
- The most copied corporate logo: the Playboy Bunny, Los Angeles.
- The largest number of buildings housing an American municipal art collection: LACMA, the Los Angeles County Museum of Art.
- The world's most expansive private art collection on public display: the Getty Center.
- Television's most popular series: Baywatch.
- The most popular American symphony conductor in Europe: Michael Tilson Thomas, San Francisco Symphony Orchestra.
- The video pornography production capital of the world: the San Fernando Valley in Los Angeles.

Even industries that surpass the California version can't ignore it. Bombay, India, produces far more films than Hollywood, California, yet India's film capital has dubbed itself 'Bollywood'.

The very concept of **film star** is a California creation, a promotional gimmick dreamt up by early film producers. The star system, which forced cinema personalities to work for specific production studios only, has disappeared, but stars themselves have prospered – think **Clint Eastwood** or **Tom Cruise**, **Sandra Bullock** or **Meryl Streep**.

California has been equally good to – and for – business. Valley of Heart's Delight, a lush valley of rolling fruit orchards just south of San Francisco, draws blank stares even from most Californians. Fast forward to the 1990s and replace the orchards with computer companies carrying names like **Apple**, **Intel** and **Hewlett-Packard**. Change the name, too, and **Silicon Valley** remains the original that high-tech entrepreneurs from Scotland to Taiwan are still trying to match.

Getting around

California is immense. Outside San Francisco, there isn't an urban area in the state that can be explored without a car. And while trains and coaches cover the 450 miles separating San Francisco and Los Angeles, they don't allow for side-trips, detours or the instant decisions that make travel more joy than journey.

Bicycles

Bicycles are a popular way to tour rural areas such as Wine Country and Yosemite National Park. Bikes are equally popular in Golden Gate Park (San Francisco), the Venice Beach Boardwalk (Los Angeles), Balboa Park (San Diego) and other urban areas. Cycles can be hired (*$–$$*) wherever they have become popular.

Accidents

Stop after any accident. Call the California Highway Patrol (**CHP**) or local police in case of injuries or physical damage. Accidents must also be reported to the car-hire company.

Collisions involving death, injury or property damage over $500 must be reported to the California Department of Motor Vehicles (**DMV**) within 10 days. DMV offices are listed in the telephone book *White Pages*. When police arrive, have your driving licence, vehicle registration, proof of insurance and contact information ready. You should exchange the same information with the other driver(s). Get the names and addresses of any witnesses.

Breakdowns

Pull off the road as far as possible, turn on the flashing hazard lights and raise the bonnet. Some highways have bright yellow emergency call boxes to telephone for help. Otherwise, dial 911 from any telephone for police or medical assistance. Check the telephone book for a tow truck (breakdown lorry).

Car-hire companies generally pay for repairs directly – ask about procedures when picking up your vehicle. If a hired car will be out of service for more than a few hours, ask for a replacement from the hire company.

Camper vans

Camper vans are called **RVs** (recreational vehicles) in the US and generally follow truck regulations, including slower speed limits (55mph). Some secondary roads restrict RVs because of hazardous driving conditions. RVs are taller than cars and more subject to being blown about by the wind and rolling over on curves. The unexpected height can cause collisions with petrol (gas) stations, toll booths, car parks, signs, trees and other obstructions.

Camping

Camping, by tent or by RV, has become so popular that advance reservations are essential. To book camping pitches in **State Parks**, contact **ParkNet** (*PO Box 1510, Rancho Cordova, CA 95741; tel: 800-444-7275*). For **National Park** bookings, contact the listed parks. Big city sporting goods stores usually have tents and other basics for hire.

Car hire

Most car-hire companies offer subcompact, economy, mid-sized, full-sized, luxury and sport utility vehicles (**SUVs**) with automatic transmission, air-conditioning and unlimited mileage. Book well in advance – rental demand often outstrips the supply of cars.

A credit card deposit is required, even if the hire has been pre-paid. Most hire companies require that drivers be aged 25 or older, though some allow younger drivers with an additional charge.

Anyone who drives a hired vehicle must be listed on the contract. If an unlisted driver has an accident, expect to pay for all repairs on your own.

Hire companies generally offer a choice: hire the vehicle with a full tank of petrol and return it full (cheaper), or hire the vehicle with a full tank of petrol, pay an inflated price for the fuel, and return it nearly empty (more expensive).

Be sure you have all registration and insurance documents before leaving the hire depot, as well as directions to your first stop. Try to spend the first night in a hotel near the airport rather than dashing from an exhausting international plane flight into a strange vehicle and new driving conditions.

Car insurance

California requires third-party liability cover, at least $15,000 for death or injury to one person, $30,000 for death or injury to more than one person and $5000 for property damage. US and Canadian drivers may be covered by their own insurance. Other renters may want to buy coverage or purchase the collision damage waiver (**CDW**), sometimes called loss damage waiver (**LDW**) offered by hire companies. Without the waiver, renters are personally liable for the full value of the vehicle. Many fly-drive packages require CDW.

Coaches

Called buses in America, motorcoaches are useful for travel between metropolitan centres, but seldom serve tourist attractions. The primary coach company in California is **Greyhound Bus Lines** (*tel: 800-231-2222*). Greyhound, like AMTRAK (trains) and some airlines, has discount passes, but offers and restrictions change frequently.

Documents

California recognises driving licences from other states and countries, but you must have the licence with you while driving.

Driving conditions

Caltrans (*tel: 800-427-7623*) has recorded highway information, listed by highway number. Check highway maps closely. No two brands of maps use the same symbols or colours for the same features.

California offers driving extremes from deep sand to heavy snow and urban traffic jams. In the **desert**, carry water, food, warm clothing and a torch. In case of trouble, raise the bonnet and *stay with your vehicle*. It's the only shade around and a car or RV is easier to spot than a person on foot. **Winter** snow can stop traffic for hours. Many mountain passes are closed late Nov–June; open highways often require tyre chains. For winter mountain trips, ask the car-hire company to include chains or buy your own (*$$*). Petrol station attendants and roadside workers install chains when needed (*$$*). Carry warm clothing, food and water in case of traffic delays and keep the petrol tank at least half full. An ice scraper and a small shovel are useful.

Hitchhiking is illegal.

DUI – drinking, drugs and driving

DUI (driving under the influence) of alcohol or other drugs, is illegal. California's blood alcohol limit, 0.01 per cent, is strictly enforced.

Fuel

Most vehicles, including RVs, take unleaded petrol; a few use diesel. Both are sold at **gas stations** (petrol stations) in US gallons (about 4 litres). Buy regular grade unless the car-hire company specifies otherwise. Most stations are self-service; some offer full service at a substantially higher price. Gas stations generally accept credit cards and $20 bills or traveller's cheques, but nothing larger.

Parking

Parking garages and parking lots (car parks) are marked by a white **P** on a blue background. Prices are posted at the entrance.

Street parking is usually limited by signs, coin-operated parking meters or kerb colours:
Red: No stopping or parking.
White: Passenger loading / unloading only.
Green: Limited parking, usually 10 minutes.
Yellow: Commercial loading zone.
Blue: Handicapped parking.

No parking within 15ft of a fire hydrant or 3ft of a kerb ramp, in bus stops, crosswalks (zebra crossings) sidewalks (pavements) or on freeways. Fines levied against hired cars are charged against your credit card.

Police

Police use flashing red and blue lights, sirens and loudhailers to signal drivers. Pull over as quickly as possible, turn off the engine and roll down the driver's side window, but don't get out unless requested. At a minimum, the officer will want to see your driving licence and vehicle registration. Police occasionally let drivers off with a warning.

Public transport

Every major city in California has a public transport system. Most are designed for commuters and do not serve tourist attractions on convenient schedules.

Road signs

European-style road signs are common, but not universal:
Red means stop, do not enter, or wrong way.
Yellow indicates warnings.
Orange marks road repairs or detours.
White shows speed limits and distances.
Brown lists parks, camping and other recreation facilities.
Blue lists local services.

Seat belts

Front-seat passengers are required to use seat belts at all times.

Speed limits

The highway speed limit is 65mph unless marked otherwise. Some freeways are marked 70mph. The limit in town is 25mph unless marked otherwise.

Trains

Rail service is generally slow, expensive and sometimes scenic. **AMTRAK** (*tel: 800-872-7245; web: http://www.amtrak.com*) operates long-distance rail services. The **Coast Starlite** runs the length of California between San Diego and Seattle, Washington. The most scenic stretch is between San Luis Obispo and Oakland (San Francisco).

TOP TEN
Don't miss

8 Death Valley National Park

California is reduced to its elemental colours and skeletal shapes in Death Valley, with the salty wastes of the lowest spot in North America within sight of snow-capped peaks. **Pages 106–107**

9 Big Sur Coast

This is the essence of Coastal California: golden mountains dropping sheer into the blue Pacific Ocean, creamy surf filling pocked-sized beaches, isolated lighthouses topping barren promontories and a single road snaking along the cliffs. **Pages 120–121**

10 Hearst Castle

This hilltop holiday home of one of America's greatest newspaper barons is proof that megalomania does have its rewards. **Page 122**

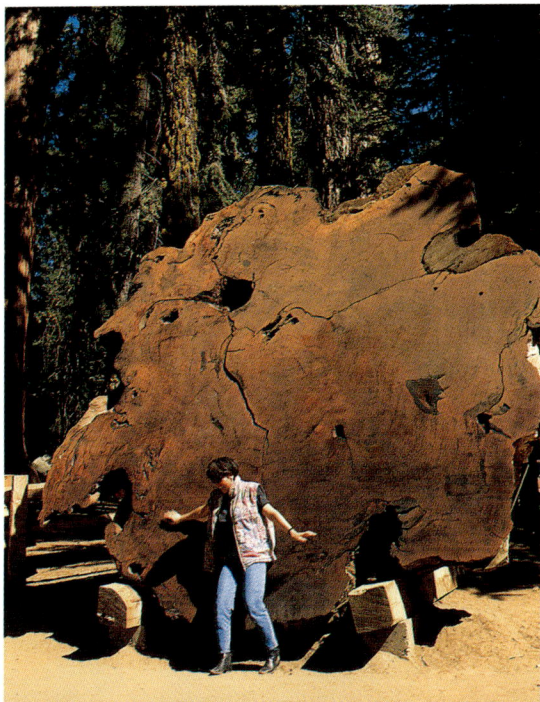

Giant redwood ☞

Los Angeles

Los Angeles hums. With cars. With life. With opportunity. The city is a mix of neighbourhoods hailing from Afghanistan to Zanzibar, 9.4 million souls dancing to the relentless rhythm of deals being cut, the underlying percussion a drumbeat of cars, sirens, machines and CD players throbbing in sync. Angelinos call their home El-Lay, a snappy moniker befitting a city of hustlers lusting to live the charmed life of a 'movie' star.

BEST OF

Los Angeles

North

| 0 | | 10 kms |
| 0 | | 5 miles |

The Getty Center

Universal City:
Universal Studios
Universal City Walk

Glendale

Beverley
Hills

Pasadena

Cinema Studio Tours

Melrose
Ave

Hollywood Blvd, Theatres, Stars, Walk of Fame

Sunset Blvd,
Hollywood to
Pacific Palisades

Hollywood History Museum

Hollywood

Rodeo Drive
Museum of
TV & Radio

George C Page Museum
La Brea Tar Pits

Olvera Street

Museum of
Tolerance

Grand Central Market

Surfrider
Beach, Malibu

Museum of
Jurassic Technology

Los
Angeles

Pier, 3rd St Promenade,
Farmers Market

Autry Museum
of the Pacific

Santa
Monica

Inglewood

Los Angeles
International
Airport

Watts Towers
of Simon Rodia

Compton

Torrance

Knott's Berry Farm

California
Island
Excursion

Disneyland

Aquarium of
the Pacific

Belmont Shores
2nd Street Scene

Santa
Ana

Long
Beach

PACIFIC
OCEAN

Queen
Mary

LOS ANGELES

① *The Getty Center*

The most visually stunning of LA's many art museums is a mountaintop castle with the city spread out at its feet. If the art and architecture don't wow you, the views (especially at sunset) will. **Page 25**

② *Grand Central Market*

All of ethnic LA flows through the Grand Central Market, usually sooner rather than later. If it's on the table between Albania and Zanzibar, it's probably on offer here. **Page 26**

③ *Griffith Park*

Birds, mountain lions and coyotes share the hills above Hollywood with joggers, cyclists, sightseers and a clutch of museums as eclectic as LA itself.
Page 26

④ *Studio tours*

Getting close to the stars and close to the action is Hollywood's ultimate insider's game. Every major cinema or television studio (and most of the minor ones) encourages visitors. **Page 29**

⑤ *Venice*

Venice, Italy, was the inspiration for Venice, California, but LA's own vision of reality has transformed the romantic original into a full-time circus. **Page 31**

" Los Angeles, like America, like freedom applied, is strong medicine – an untidy jumble of human diversity and perversity. "

**Political commentator
George Will**

Tourist information

Los Angeles Convention & Visitors Bureau (LACVB) (*tel: 800-228-2452*) has a 24-hour events hotline (*tel: 213-689-8822; web: www.lacvb.com*) and two visitor centres: **Downtown** *685 S Figueroa St between Wilshire Blvd and 7th St. Open Mon–Fri 0800–1700, Sat 0830–1700*; **Hollywood Visitor Information Center** *The Janes House, 6541 Hollywood Blvd. Open Mon–Sat 0900–1700*. Ask for the guides *Destination Los Angeles, Shopping, Dining & Nightlife and Entertainment*. LA without a car isn't realistic. The MTA, public transport, is legendary for inefficiency and poor service.

Aquarium of the Pacific

100 Aquarium Way, Long Beach. Tel: 562-590-3100; web: aquariumofpacific.org. Open daily 1000–1800. Admission: $$.

The world's best chance to encounter the Pacific Ocean in one spot: 10,000 individual creatures in three sets of tanks recreating the sub-Arctic Bering Sea, Southern and Baja California's temperate, kelp-rich waters and tropical coral lagoons from Palau, in Micronesia. Don't miss the **outdoor touch tank** on the upper level.

Autry Museum of Western Heritage

4700 Western Heritage Way, Griffith Park. Tel: 323-667-2000; web: www.autry-museum.org. Open Tue–Sun 1000–1700. Admission: $$.

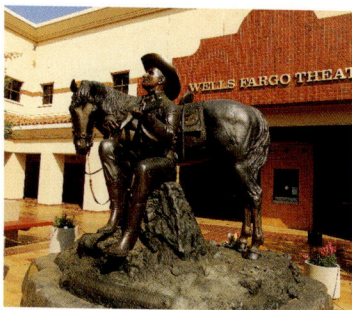

Gene Autry, the 'Singing Cowboy' film star, left behind a candid, comprehensive look at America's Old West. Beyond the Hollywood artefacts lies a truer Wild West, from Spanish *conquistadors'* encounters with Native Americans to the silver-studded and spurred *vaqueros*, who evolved into the range-riding, buckskin-garbed cowboys. There are impressive displays of historic Colt firearms.

Disneyland

1313 Harbor Blvd, Anaheim. Tel: 714-781-4565; web: www.disneyland.com. Open daily, hours variable. Admission: $$$.

Half a century on, Walt Disney's formula of themed lands with rides, costumed cartoon and film characters and trademark souvenirs still enthrals millions. Enter and exit the park at **Main Street, U.S.A.**, an idealised version of small-town America *circa* 1910. The **Main Street Cinema** plays *Steamboat Willie*, Disney's original 1928 version of Mickey Mouse. Mouse ears, Mouse balloons, Mouse souvenirs – they're all for sale on Main Street.

Travertine *redux*

The travertine limestone tiles that cover the Getty Center were cut to display the holes, fissures and fossils that occur naturally in the stone. Roman and Renaissance stonecutters, who used the same quarry, laboured to hide the faults that modern architects so prize.

Adventureland stars the **Indiana Jones Adventure**, an archaeological adventure snatched from the jaws of success. **Sleeping Beauty's Castle** is the entrance to **Fantasyland**, where fairy tales spring to life. **Mickey's Toontown** has cartoon-based attractions for the very young.

Frontierland evokes 19th-century America, including the hardly *risqué* **Pirates of the Caribbean** and the **Haunted Mansion** fun house of horrors. **Tomorrowland's** retro-futuristic design incorporates a Leonardo da Vinci astrolabe. Find an early viewing spot for the Main Street U.S.A. evening parade and fireworks over Sleeping Beauty's Castle.

Disney is building a second theme park, **Disney's California Adventure**, next to the original Disneyland. Expect traffic and construction delays throughout 2001.

The Getty Center

1200 Getty Center Dr off I-405. Tel: 310-440-7300; web: www.getty.edu. Open Sat–Sun 1000–1800, Tue–Wed 1100–1900, Thur–Fri 1100–2100. Admission and passenger drop-off free, but reservation-required parking, $.

The Getty is how oil billionaires (and their estates) spend their spare cash. Distinctive wavy-line exterior walls covered with the same travertine limestone used for the Colosseum and St Peter's Basilica in Rome frame stunning views of LA to the Pacific Ocean. Refreshing courtyards, seasonal gardens, 600 acres of naturally landscaped grounds and inexpensive restaurants vie with an eclectic collection that mixes masterpieces with over-indulgence. From photographs to illuminated medieval manuscripts, the Getty takes in the past 12 centuries of Western, mostly European, Art. A quick-tour brochure outlines a one-hour 'best of' overview. Do not miss the sunset views across LA.

Grand Central Market

317 S Broadway, Downtown. Tel: 213-624-2378. Open Mon–Sat 0900–1800, Sun 1000–1730. 90 min free parking with a $15 purchase.

Fishmongers, butchers, greengrocers, bakers and assorted snack vendors have been selling ethnic foodstuffs here since 1917. The dominant flavour is Latino, the Mexican-Central American-South American culture that dominates LA's outlying neighbourhoods, but the ethnic mix is as eclectic as LA itself. Grand Central's fresh-squeezed juice bars are a refreshing stop before heading across Hill St to take the Victorian-style **Angels Flight funicular** up to Bunker Hill skyscrapers.

Griffith Park

Griffith Park Ranger Visitor Center, 4730 Crystal Springs Dr. Tel: 323-665-5188; web: www.griffithobs.org/Hall.html. Park free; some attractions charge.

Join Angelinos in their century-old green haven in the Santa Monica Mountains above Hollywood. Birds, mountain lions and deer wandering in fern glens and oak groves share the park with the **Los Angeles Zoo** (*5333 Zoo Dr; tel: 323-644-4200; web: www.lazoo.org; admission: $$*), equestrians, golfers and pop-music lovers at open-air **Greek Theater** concerts (*2700 N Vermont Ave; tel: 323-665-1927; admission: $$$*) and the **Autry Museum of Western Heritage** (*see page 24*).

Griffith Observatory (*2800 E Observatory Rd; tel: 323-664-1191*) may be LA's best above-the-sprawl sunset-watching venue, complete with free admission to the star-and-planet **Hall of Science** (*open daily 1230–2200 summer and weekends, Tue–Fri 1400–2200 winter*). The **telescope** is open for viewing (*Tue–Sun 1900–2145 winter, dark–2145 summer*).

Up in the air

Smog may be LA's most famous product, but air pollution isn't unique to the modern era. Spanish explorer Juan Rodríguez Cabrillo named the grand curve of the Los Angeles coast 'Bay of Smokes' for the dark haze of campfire smoke that hung over the basin – in 1542.

Hollywood History Museum

1660 N Highland Ave, Hollywood. Tel: 323-464-7776. Open daily. Admission: $$.

This jewel-like art-deco building was once headquarters for the Max Factor make-up and cosmetics empire. The museum displays posters, costumes and 'movie' equipment employed to create the magic of Hollywood's silent film era, talkies and today's whiz-bam-zap technology.

Knott's Berry Farm

8039 Beach Blvd, Buena Park. Tel: 714-220-5220; web: www.knotts.com. Open daily, call for hours. Admission: $$.

This all-American theme park began as a chicken restaurant opened by a berry farm family to survive the 1930s economic disaster. Beyond the nostalgic, if hardly outstanding, American farm cuisine is a thrilling assortment of roller coasters in six theme areas. The Wild West and Native American areas are surprisingly authentic, a tribute to the founder's collection of Western buildings and care to depict Indians with cultural accuracy.

Roller coasters are fast, lurching, twisting and spiralling almost faster than the happy adrenalin-charged screams. **GhostRider** is the longest and tallest wooden roller coaster in Southern California. **Montezooma's Revenge** accelerates to 55mph in less than 4 seconds. Harnessed riders rise 300ft skyward, then plummet to earth in 3 seconds of raw terror on **Supreme Scream**.

George C Page Museum – La Brea Tar Pits

5801 Wilshire Blvd. Tel: 213-934-7243; web: www.tarpits.org. Open Tue–Fri 0930–1700, Sat–Sun 1000–1700. Admission: $.

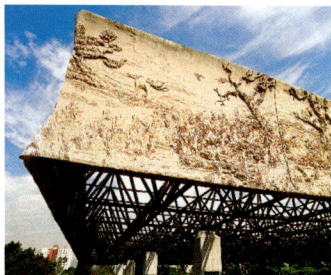

If LA looks new, look again. Bubbling tar pits along Wilshire Blvd's Museum Row have yielded fossils, 40,000-year-old Ice Age relics, more than 1.5 million bones and one female human skeleton. Mastodons, sabre-toothed cats, giant sloths and wolves arrayed around the museum's perimeter bas-relief hint at the fossil exhibits inside.

Olvera Street

Downtown. Open daily 1000–1900. Free. Sepulveda House Visitor's Center open Mon–Sat 1000–1500.

Tourist Mexico meets Los Angeles on Olvera St, officially **El Pueblo de Los Angeles Historic Monument**. Two blocks of covered booths line the centre of this pedestrian street, with Mexican-crafted leather bags and belts, dolls, blouses, serape blankets, rugs and other souvenirs enhanced by roving *mariachi* bands.

Los Angeles was founded here in 1781, evolving a lifestyle depicted with fictional flair in several 'Zorro' films. The reality lies in LA's oldest building, the perfectly restored **1818 Avila Adobe**. **Los Angelinas del Pueblo** offers free park walking tours (*130 Paseo de la Plaza; tel: 213-628-1274; tours Tue–Sat 1000–1300*).

The *Queen Mary*

1126 Queens Hwy, Long Beach. Tel: 562-435-3511; web: www.queenmary.com. Open daily 1000–1800. Admission: $$.

What was once the most elegant vessel afloat has been fitted out as a luxury hotel, with many of the teak-lined first-class areas refurbished for tours. Tour a Russian Soviet-era **Scorpion submarine** (*next to the Queen Mary; tel: 562-435-3511; open daily 1000–1800; admission: $$*).

Santa Monica

Santa Monica Visitor Center, 1400 Ocean Ave, Santa Monica. Tel: 310-393-7593; web: www.santamonica.com. Open daily 1000–1600.

The **Santa Monica Pier** (*end of Colorado Ave*) sports a restaurant with views up the curving coastline towards Malibu, amusement rides, an historic carousel and plenty of benches for watching the waves roll by. Alfresco cafés, boutiques, bar-restaurants and whimsical topiary animals juice up the youthful verve of the **Third Street Promenade** (*Third St from Wilshire Blvd–Broadway*). A Wednesday and Saturday **Farmer's Market** (*Third St Promenade at Arizona Ave*) is filled with red and green peppers, squashes, crimson tomatoes, flowers and unpretentious film stars shopping for dinner.

Studio tours

Star-struck? Star-gazing? Consult the daily schedule in the *Shoot Sheet for Television, Film, Commercial Advertisement, and Video Filming* from the **Entertainment Industry Development Council Film Office** (*7083 Hollywood Blvd, Ste 500; tel: 323-957-1000; open Mon–Fri 0830–1800; $$; or browse free on-line: web: www.eidc.com/community/shoot.html*).

Audiences Unlimited (*tel: 818-506-0067 or 818-753-3470*) distributes free tickets to television studio tapings. Over 9 years old? **Paramount Studios** (*5555 Melrose Ave, Hollywood; tel: 323-956-1777 or 323-956-5575*) offer walking tours (*Mon–Fri 0900–1400; admission: $$*). **Universal Studios Hollywood Backlot Tour** (*Universal City; tel: 818-508-9600; admission: $$$*) is LA's theme park highlight. **Warner Bros Studio VIP Tour** (*4000 Warner Blvd, Burbank; tel: 818-972-8687 or 818-954-1744; open Mon–Fri 0900–1500 Oct–May, to 1600 June–Sept; admission: $$*) is a cart-drawn adventure.

Sunset Boulevard

Sunset Boulevard traces half the width of LA, from the beach through the lower Santa Monica Mountains nearly to downtown. Neon and oversized billboards flash trendy adverts for the latest music stars and film hits along **Sunset Strip** (*7800–9200 Sunset Blvd*) in **West Hollywood**. The beat throbs into the wee hours in clubs like the atmospheric, almost sleazy **Viper Room** (*8852 Sunset Blvd; tel: 310-358-1880*) co-owned by actor Johnny Depp. The **Chateau Marmont** (*8221 Sunset Blvd; tel: 323-656-1010*) has been home away from home for stars from Garbo to Jagger.

Will Rogers State Historic Park (*1501 Will Rogers State Park Rd, Pacific Palisades; tel: 310-454-8212; admission: $*), off the west end of Sunset Boulevard, preserves the 1924–35 home, stables and polo field of the beloved humorist, broadcaster and actor just north of the posh enclave of Pacific Palisades. Trails and equestrian paths lead to superb vantage points in the Santa Monica Mountains.

Surfrider beach

Pacific Coast Hwy (Hwy 1), Malibu.

It's just a few hundred yards of sand out of 18 miles-worth of surfing and sunning beaches along Hwy 1, the Pacific Coast Hwy, north of Santa Monica, but dedicated surfers call it the centre of the universe. Surfers know Surfrider as the original surfing beach in Southern California, but the area is better known as Malibu, a favoured beachside colony for cinema stars since the 1920s.

Universal Studios

100 Universal City Plaza, Universal City. Tel: 818-622-3801; web: www.universalstudios.com/unicity2/ush.html. Open daily, call for hours. Admission: $$$.

Universal, one of the world's oldest film studios, is surrounded by a cinema-themed amusement park and LA's theme-park version of itself, CityWalk. Universal feels more adult than other area theme

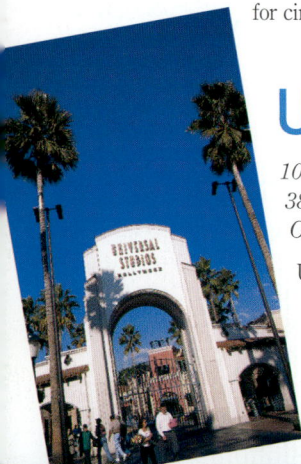

parks, with its **Backlot Tram Tour** (*see page 29*), a good introduction to film-making. Then experience waves of flame from **Backdraft**, lava flows in **Back to the Future – The Ride** and a morphed leap-from-the-screen ultimate villain in **Terminator 2 3-D**.

Universal CityWalk, outside the park entrance, is a walking street for shopping before dining and evening club entertainment at the **Hard Rock Café Hollywood** (*$$*), **B.B. King's Blues Club** (*$$*), and **Wizardz Magic Club and Dinner Theatre** (*$$*).

Venice

The beach scene revolves around the **Venice Boardwalk**, a winding pedestrian, bicycle, skate, dog-and-everything-else path running south from Santa Monica towards Los Angeles International Airport. At its peak at weekends and summer near Venice Beach Recreation Center (*foot of Windward Ave*), a free-form circus rules over an amorphous crowd of exhibitionists, musicians and magicians, jugglers, street preachers and buskers. Oozing good form and taut muscles, the best-of-the-best flaunt their stuff at **Muscle Beach** (*Windward Ave at 19th Ave*), a legendary outdoor body-building studio.

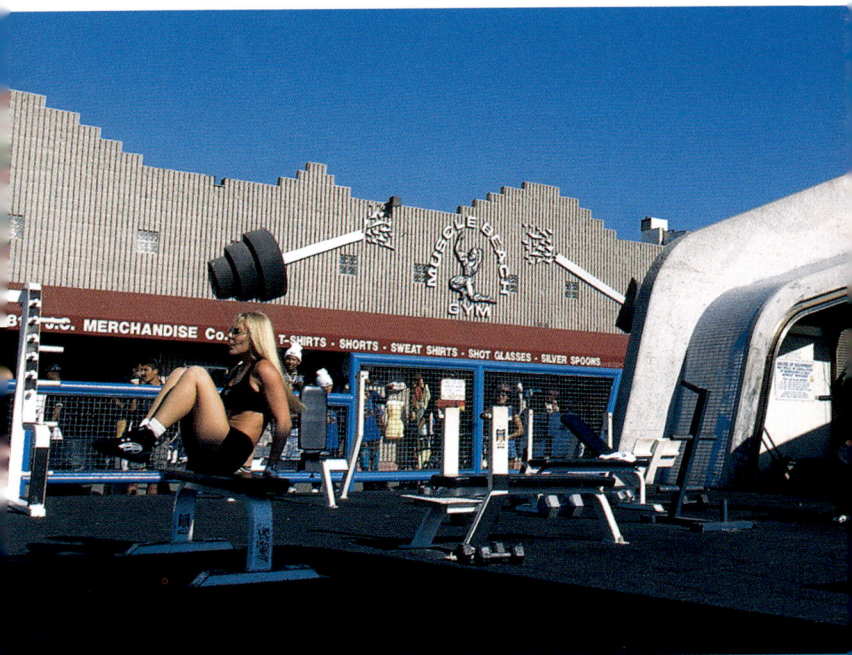

Eating out

Foodies are a privileged class in LA. Just ask superstar chefs like Wolfgang Puck. Or consult the inexpensive burgundy-coloured pocket-sized Zagat Survey Los Angeles, *the best restaurant guide to LA. Dining, current clubs, nightlife and concerts are up to date in the free newspapers,* LA Weekly, New Times Los Angeles *and* Entertainment Today, *in news stands around the city, and in the mainstream* Los Angeles Times *Sunday* Calendar *and Thursday* Weekend *sections.*

Canter's Restaurant

419 N Fairfax Ave, near Beverly Blvd. Tel: 323-651-2030. $. One of LA's oldest, most famous, most crowded and best delicatessens.

O2 Restaurant

8788 Sunset Blvd, West Hollywood. Tel: 310-360-9002. $$. Actor Woody Harrelson's venture into the macrobiotic world with all-natural, all-raw selections is in a vaguely 1960s psychedelic setting. No alcohol, but hookahs in the back room oxygen lounge dispense pure oxygen in several flavours.

The Original Pantry Café

877 S Figueroa St. Tel: 213-972-9279. $. Old-timers claim it has never been closed and never without customers since it opened downtown in 1924.

Papadakis Taverna

301 W 6th St, San Pedro. Tel: 310-548-1186. $$$. The best Greek restaurant in Greater LA despite touristy plate smashing and belly dancing.

Restaurante Guelaguetza

3337 1/2 8th St. Tel: 213-427-0601. $. One of LA's most authentic Mexican restaurants specialises in *molé* and other specialities from Oaxaca.

Spago

176 N Canon Dr, Beverly Hills. Tel: 310-385-0880. $$$. Puck's flagship eatery is no longer extraordinary, but watching Hollywood's biggest stars and most anxious wannabes playing to each other and to the waiting paparazzi is. Advance bookings are essential.

Tommy's

2575 W Beverly Blvd. Tel: 213-389-9060. $. The place for greasy, gloppy and absolutely the greatest chilli burgers and *tamales.*

Wolfgang Puck Café

Multiple locations. $$. The Spago offshoots serve the same dishes for less than half the Beverly Hills price and with none of the attitude.

Shopping

Shoppers, you haven't died and gone to heaven, you've just gone to LA. Malls are all the rage, indoor, outdoor and fly-by-night. For ethnic buys, shop ethnic neighbourhoods: Chinatown, Little Tokyo, Koreatown, etc.

The Fashion District

7th St to I-10 (Santa Monica Fwy), Broadway to San Pedro. Tel: 213-488-1153; web: www.dpoa.com.

Saturday is bargain day, but shoppers can pick up samples at rock-bottom prices on the last Friday of the month. There are wholesale outlets to the 'rag' trade and vendors who retail to the public, so check that it's a retail store before entering, then be prepared for bargains. The indoor **CaliforniaMart** (*110 E 9th St; tel: 213-630-3600*) has remarkable variety. Street-level **Santee Alley** (*between Santee St and Maple Ave Olympic Blvd–11th St*) is an adventure into an ethnic pedestrian street peopled by mannequins.

Nightlife

On Friday or Saturday night Melrose Avenue is kerb-to-kerb stretch limousines and valet parking. The strip that television show *Melrose Place* put on the map remains a scene for be-seen dining, punk-grunge boutiques and shocking shopfront décor. Drink in the ultra-cool, almost hip attitude which the daytime denizens project, then search after dark for their dressed-all-in-black cousins discreetly flirting with film-star handsome car valets.

Say it ain't Kryptonite!

When television's first Superman leapt over tall buildings in a single bound in the 1950s, the signature white tower he surmounted was LA City Hall. The building is currently closed for seismic retrofitting.

Hollywood

Hollywood (Hollywood Blvd between Gower and Vine Sts) *is still a little sleazy, with showgirl flimsies and mules in shop windows, street people hanging around and aspiring actors everywhere – but Hollywood evokes the magic of cinema and the allure of stardom.*

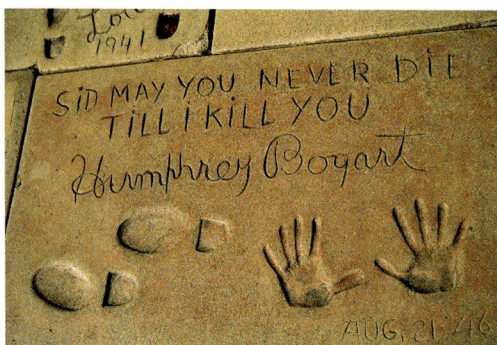

So do the gigantic letters spelling HOLLYWOOD just below the crest of the Santa Monica Mountains that loom north of the town-that-is-a-neighbourhood. Egos are never restrained in what was already the Movie Capital of the World before Charlie Chaplin and other British arrivals added their own genius to the mix. Generations of film, television, radio, music and stage luminaries are celebrated with more than 2000 pink and bronze stars set into the pavement along the **Hollywood Boulevard Walk of Fame** from La Brea Ave to Vine St.

The blazing orange signs of the **Hollywood History Walk** (*tel: 323- 463-6767; web: www.hollywoodbid.org*) create a coherent glimpse of Hollywood's glory days of yesteryear with stops at 16 historic buildings and sites, most of them along Hollywood Boulevard.

Two of the world's grandest cinema palaces are here: **Mann's Chinese Theater** (*6925 Hollywood Blvd; tel: 323-464-8111*), its entrance courtyard filled with decades worth of film stars' autographed hand and footprints below an exotic pagoda façade; and the American Cinemateque's recently restored

Hooray for Hollywood

Hollywood began as 'Hollywoodland', a 1923 tract of elegant Spanish Mediterranean homes. Developers erected a white sign with letters 50ft tall by 30ft wide to publicise the new neighbourhood. The sign fell into disrepair and the last syllable was torn down in the 1950s. The famous name, 'Hollywood', is best seen from the Griffith Park Observatory.

1922 **Egyptian Theater** (*6712 Hollywood Blvd; tel: 323-777-3456*) with regular screenings of classic Hollywood films off a Roaring 20s version of an Egyptian temple courtyard, replete with wall murals, palm trees and a fountain.

Frederick's of Hollywood Lingerie Museum (*6608 Hollywood Blvd; tel: 323-466-8506; web: www.fredericks.com/museum*) is a charming, almost *risqué* peek at what stars and lesser beauties have worn since 1947 when the eponymous Mr Frederick decided that what suited Hollywood's glam gals would be scooped up by American housewives. Madonna's *bustier* is a star attraction.

San Francisco

San Francisco is The City, studded with steep hills, surrounded by the waters of a magnificent bay on two sides and the Pacific Ocean surf on a third. The Golden Gate Bridge glistens, cable cars climb halfway to the stars and fog fills the air. This world-beloved city is cosmopolitan, from North Beach coffee-houses to exotic Chinatown, and the polyglot of languages and cuisines in between.

SAN FRANCISCO

BEST OF
San Francisco

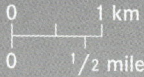

0 — 1 km
0 — ½ mile

North

SAN FRANCISCO BAY

4 Golden Gate Bridge
Fort Point

Exploratorium

Bay Cruise

National Maritime Museum

1 Alcatraz
5 Pier 39 Sea Lions

Ghirardelli Square

Chestnut Street Scene

Chestnut Street
Lombard Street

North Beach

Coit Tower Telegraph Hill

3

101

Palace of Fine Arts

6 Cable Car Ride

2

Lombard Street

Cable Car Barn & Museum

Washington Square

Chinatown

Presidio

Victorian Homes

Masonic Avenue

Van Ness Avenue

Grace Cathedral

Barbary Coast Trail

Treasure Island Cityscape

I

California Street

Union Square Shopping

Old US Mint

80

95

Market Street

101

Cartoon Art Museum

Japanese Tea Garden

Soma District

Historic Street Cars to the Castro District

Fell Street

Haight Street

Haight Street

Golden Gate Park

Market Street

101

280

Twin Peaks View

Mission District Murals

Castro District

SAN FRANCISCO

① Alcatraz Island

Solitary confinement on this tiny shark-surrounded island 1^1/$_2$ miles off shore made this almost escape-proof penitentiary notorious for being within sight but out of reach of civilisation. **Page 40**

② Cable cars

San Francisco's thrill rides masquerade as public transport. Open-sided cable cars haul over hills from Market Street's department stores to Fisherman's Wharf via Union Square, Nob Hill, Chinatown and North Beach or to the Financial District. **Page 41**

③ 49-Mile Drive

A driving tour to take in all the highlights and vistas of the hills to the Pacific Ocean, this seagull-sign route is one of the world's best-designed half-day introductions to a city. **Page 43**

④ Golden Gate Bridge

Two graceful towers rising orange above the mouth of San Francisco Bay were an architectural wonder in 1938, and today are the city's most recognisable landmark. Millions of visitors walk or bicycle across the bridge each year to drink in views of San Francisco's boat-bedecked Bay, side by side with residents commuting to Marin County. **Page 44**

⑤ Pier 39 sea lions

An old pier becomes a dining and shopping venue and pinniped squatters take over the adjacent marina. Barking sea lions, massive and noble, move in, 600 strong, for most of the year, within easy swimming distance of Alcatraz and the Golden Gate Bridge. **Page 45**

⑥ Lombard Street

Famed as the 'crookedest street in the world', this block-long one-way serpentine road plunges down from San Francisco's hilly heights into the heart of North Beach. **Page 45**

Getting around

Walk. One-way streets and steep hills are driving nightmares.

Muni (*tel: 415-673-6864*) service is erratic. **Buses** follow numbered routes. **Streetcars**, sometimes running underground, are lettered. **Cable cars** serve Nob Hill, Fisherman's Wharf, Aquatic Park and California St. **BART** (Bay Area Rapid Transit District) (*tel: 510-992-2278*) runs from San Francisco to the East Bay. **Blue & Gold Fleet** (*tel: 415-705-5555*) access the East Bay, Alcatraz, Angel Island and bay sightseeing. **Golden Gate Ferry** (*tel: 415-923-2000*) serves Marin County's Sausalito and Tiburon.

Tourist information

San Francisco Convention & Visitor Bureau (SFCVB) *Hallidie Plaza, Lower Level, Powell and Market Sts. Tel: 415-391-2000; web: www.sfvisitor.org. Open Mon–Fri 0900–1700, Sat–Sun 0900–1500. For 24-hour recorded information: tel: 415-391-2001.*

Alcatraz Island

Access by Blue & Gold ferry. Tel: 415-556-0560. Open daily. Admission: $$.

The Rock, part of Golden Gate National Recreation Area, has never lacked for visitors, though few of them came by choice until recent years. The list of prisoners who spent time at the infamous federal penitentiary reads like a *Who's Who* of celebrity criminals. **Al 'Scarface' Capone**, **Robert 'Bird Man of Alcatraz' Stroud** and **George 'Machine Gun' Kelly** were among the 1554 convicts who spent an average of eight years within sight of San Francisco.

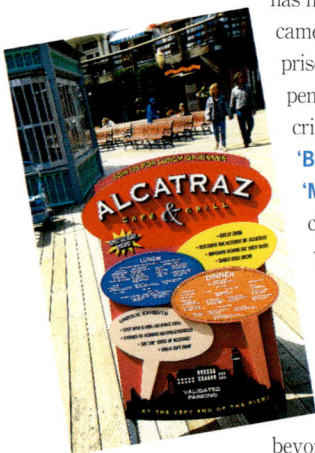

The tiny island is $1^1/_2$ miles off shore and surrounded, in popular myth anyway, by ravenous sharks. Ripped by relentless winds, washed by fierce tides and hovering just beyond the fleshpots of San Francisco, prison life was calculated to drive inmates to despair.

Blue & Gold Fleet operate daily tours of the prison that has probably been glorified in more films than any other. Wander the cellblocks, and step into the 'dark holes', solitary confinement cells used liberally as punishment pens. The **self-guided audio tour** (*$*), narrated by former prison guards, evokes the dank atmosphere of what was long heralded as America's only 'escape proof' prison. Only 36 cons ever fled: 10 were killed trying; 21 were recaptured and 5 disappeared.

Barbary Coast Trail

Walk on 150 years of raucous San Francisco history in 3.8 miles from the Old Mint (vacant because of seismic problems) to Aquatic Park. Most of the 150 bronze plaques set into the pavement depict Gold Rush-era events and personalities, but there's something for just about every interest: twenty historic sites, six museums, pubs, outdoor cafés and panoramic views. The SFCVB publish free trail guides; history buffs can explore in more detail with the *Barbary Coast Trail Official Guide* (*$*) or *Walking San Francisco on the Barbary Coast Trail* (*$$*).

Bay cruises

To escape from the concrete canyons of downtown and feel the vast sweep of San Francisco Bay, take a bay tour. Budget-watchers should jump aboard a commuter ferry. **Blue & Gold Fleet** (*tel: 415-705-5555; fare: $$*) do circle tours, cruising under the **Golden Gate Bridge** and the **San Francisco-Oakland Bay Bridge** close to **Alcatraz**, **Angel Island**, **Treasure Island** and the **San Francisco waterfront**.

Cable cars

Tel: 415-673-6864. Fare: $.

Cars still climb **Nob Hill** between the Bay and Hallidie Plaza (*Powell and Market Sts*) and along **California St**. The **Hyde St Line** runs to **Aquatic Park** (*Beach St between Hyde St and Van Ness Ave*) for easy access to **Fisherman's Wharf** and the historic ships at **Hyde St Pier** in **San Francisco Maritime National Historic Park**.

There are two ways to ride a cable car. Queue up (for hours in summer) to board at the terminus of each cable car line, or, more expeditiously, walk a couple of blocks up the street to climb aboard as San Franciscans do.

To see how the mechanical system actually works, stop at the **Cable Car Barn Gallery** (*Mason and Washington Sts; tel: 415-474-1887*). Below the overlook, three sets of 14ft pulleys haul miles of steel cable at a constant 9mph beneath city streets to power the cable cars, as they have since 1887. In one corner of the Barn, the **Cable Car Museum** (*$*) has maps, drawings and the remains of antique cars to bring cable-car history to life.

" *I left my heart*
In San Francisco
High on a hill
It calls to me.
To be where little cable cars
Climb halfway to the stars . . . "

– as sung by Tony Bennett

Castro district

Blocks surrounding Castro and Market Sts.

Arrive in America's most flamboyant gay neighbourhood via Muni's F (*Market St*) line, riding one of the city's **Historic Street Cars**, brilliantly restored vintage trolley cars from Lisbon, Melbourne and other cities. The all-time favourite is a canary-yellow boat car that once carried holiday-makers in Blackpool. Keep an eye out for the **Sisters of Perpetual Indulgence**, a community service group of men dressed in nuns' habits, and lavishly restored Victorian-era homes.

Chestnut Street

The Marina District's perennially up-and-coming shopping, eating and bar-hopping neighbourhood habituées are young, footloose and looking for an upmarket alternative to Goth and Punk in SOMA (South of Market Area) clubs.

Chinatown

Pine St to North Beach between Kearny and Powell Sts.

A shanty town of Chinese miners expelled from the 1860s gold fields has become the largest Chinese community outside Asia, seen each Chinese New Year when the world's longest Golden Dragon dances at the end of a television broadcast seen by millions.

On Spofford Alley, **Sun Yat Sen** planned the revolution that became the Chinese Nationalist Republic, and Chinatown favours Taiwanese politics even today. **Amy Tan's** best-selling novel, *The Joy Luck Club*, put Waverly Place, a modest side alley, on the map. Despite its ominous name, Hang Ah Alley has cheerful *dim sum* (filled dumplings).

Grant Ave is Chinatown's bow to tourism, with souvenir shops and pricey restaurants. Find *real* Chinatown a block west on Stockton St, where shoppers use elbows efficiently to find the best fresh produce, live fish, barbecued ducks and squares of raw tofu (soybean curd). Join local Chinese for plates of *dim sum*, a bowl of noodles or a lotus-and-sesame bun from a Chinese bakery.

Coit Tower

1 Telegraph Hill Blvd. Bus: 39. Tel: 415-362-0808. Open daily. Admission: $.

The 212ft nozzle-shaped tower that appears as a phallic extension atop **Telegraph Hill** was built by Lillie Coit, a turn-of-the-century city socialite with a well-known fondness for burly firemen. Splendid Depression-era murals are within and the rooftop view is spectacular.

Exploratorium

Palace of Fine Arts, 3601 Lyon St at Marina Blvd. Tel: 415-561-0362. Open Labor Day–Memorial Day Tue–Sun 1000–1700, Wed to 2130, closed Mon; Memorial Day–Labor Day daily 1000–1800, Wed to 2130. Admission: $$.

Kids get lost in the stampede of adults who can't wait to get their hands on the 500 do-it-yourself exhibits. In the **Tactile Dome**, you touch-manoeuvre through a maze of shapes and textures in utter blackness. The Exploratorium adjoins the ruddy golden **Palace of Fine Arts**, a classical Beaux Arts shell created for the 1915 Panama–Pacific Exposition.

Fort Point

Beneath the south end of the Golden Gate Bridge. Open daily.

Waves sweep through the **Golden Gate** under the bridge blasting spray 30ft into the air, challenging tourists and surfers alike. The graceful red-brick fort was built to defend San Francisco during the American Civil War. Costumed guides recreate army life from 1861 to 1865, when defenders prepared for an attack that never came.

> **❝** *It is an odd thing, but everyone who disappears is said to be seen at San Francisco. It must be a delightful city, and possess all the attractions of the next world.* **❞**
>
> **Oscar Wilde,**
> ***The Picture of Dorian Gray***

49-Mile Drive

The blue-and-white seagull signs have been updated occasionally, but the route has changed almost not at all since its inception for visitors to the 1939 Golden Gate International Exposition. The 49-Mile Drive still crams the top sights and the best views into a single itinerary. Follow the SFCVB's *49-Mile Drive* brochure. Allow at least half a day, avoiding downtown during commuter hours.

Golden Gate Bridge

Hwy 101 between San Francisco and Marin County. $ for vehicles.

Painted orange for visibility in heavy fog, the 1938 span closes the gap above the tides raging through the Golden Gate, named for Istanbul's Golden Horn. Park at the San Francisco end to walk or cycle across (free), or drive to the viewpoint at the north end of the bridge to look back toward San Francisco (pay toll driving southbound).

Golden Gate Park

Stanyan St between Fulton St and Lincoln Ave to the Pacific Ocean.

Modelled on New York City's Central Park, America's second great urban park shelters museums and open space. Take jasmine tea with fortune cookies amidst exquisite landscaping and a half-sphere moon bridge in the **Japanese Tea Garden**'s oasis of calm (*open daily; admission: $*). Next door are two museums with the same hours and single admission. The **Asian Art Museum** (*tel: 415-379-8801; web: www.asianart.org; open Wed–Sun 0930–1700; free first Wed of every month 0930–2045; admission: $$*) adjoins the **M H de Young Memorial Museum** (*tel: 415-863-3330; web: www.thinker.org*). The de Young attracts more attention for the steel girders shoring up the building's exterior from earthquake damage than for its American art from the 17th to 20th centuries and other collections.

Steepest streets

Taking the vertical plunge prize with a 31.5 per cent grade: Filbert St between Leavenworth and Hyde Sts; 22nd St between Church and Vicksburg Sts. Runner-up: 29 per cent grade – Jones St between Union and Filbert Sts.

Included in a single admission to the **California Academy of Sciences** (*$$*) are the **Steinhart Aquarium**, **Morrison Planetarium** and the **Natural History Museum** (*tel: 415-750-7145; web: www.calacademy.org; open daily Memorial Day weekend–Labor Day 0900–1800, 1000–1700 the rest of the year; free first Wed each month*). The Aquarium's crocodile pit is a lively throwback to when the most fearsome Jaws were reptilian. Seals and sea lions bark and swim entrancingly – and less odoriferously than their wild cousins at **Pier 39**. Join a free daily walk (*1330, plus 1030 at weekends*) among 17 garden habitats in **Strybing Arboretum & Botanical Gardens** (*9th Ave at Lincoln Way; tel: 415-661-1316; open Mon–Fri 0800–1630, Sat–Sun 1000–1700; free*).

Haight-Ashbury

Blocks surrounding Haight St between Masonic and Stanyan Sts, near Golden Gate Park.

The Haight was the navel of the Hippie universe in the late 1960s and early 1970s. The neighbourhood's latest reincarnation is a trendier-than-thou mix of fashion, food and body-piercing for men, women and the undecided.

Lombard Street

Between Hyde and Leavenworth Sts.

With only **eight hairpin turns** in a single 5mph block, 'crookedest street in the world' is probably hyperbole. Homeowners vie to create the most profuse front garden along the single-track red-brick street, creating a splendid panorama up the hill, especially in the morning. The view from the cable car stop at the top extends from Alcatraz to Coit Tower and beyond.

Mission District murals

One square mile east from Mission Dolores.

Brilliant acrylic **murals** reflect refugees' nostalgia for their native countries in one of America's finest collection of wall art. Seek out **Balmy Alley** for a wall reflecting the latest politics in district residents' Latin American homelands. Mexican, Hispanic and Asian restaurants thrive in a vibrant neighbourhood named after San Francisco's original 1776 church (basilica), **Mission Dolores** (*17th and Dolores Sts*).

National Maritime Historic Park

Beach St between Hyde St and Van Ness Ave. Tel: 415-556-3002. Open daily. $.

America's only floating National Park is anchored by the gleaming white art-deco streamlined building that looks like a ship, the **Maritime Museum**. The water-based park section has historic ships docked at the **Hyde Street Pier**. The square-rigged *Balclutha* and a former San Francisco Bay ferry, the *Eureka*, are open to explore.

North Beach

Blocks surrounding Broadway and Columbus Ave.

First settled by Portuguese and Italian fishermen before land-fill drove the shoreline northwards to Fisherman's Wharf, North Beach has been an entertainment and nightlife district for more than a century. Carol Doda modelled a topless bathing costume at **The Condor** (*300 Columbus Ave*) – now a sports bar – in the 1960s, starting the topless and nude-dancing craze still alive and well along Broadway's neon strip. The Beatnik era survives at poet Lawrence Ferlinghetti's **City Lights Bookstore** (*261 Columbus Ave; tel: 415-362-8193*) and **Vesuvio Café** (*255 Columbus Ave; tel: 415-362-3370; $*).

Treasure Island

East of San Francisco via Hwy 80 on the San Francisco–Oakland Bay Bridge.

The man-made island and former naval base was created for the 1939 Golden Gate International Exposition on a sand bar extending from the rocky Yerba Buena Island. The large *art-moderne* building facing San Francisco was the control tower, passenger terminal and offices for Pan American Airways' flying-boat service to Asia. Treasure Island's uncrowded public park has spectacular morning and sunset **views of the San Francisco waterfront**.

> " *A mad city – inhabited for the most part by perfectly insane people whose women are of remarkable beauty.* "
> **Rudyard Kipling**

Twin Peaks

Top of Twin Peaks Rd, off Market St.

The top of San Francisco has the best view over the entire city. Afternoon vistas are best, but beware the chill winds whipping off the Pacific Ocean and over the hilltop.

Victorian homes

The 'Painted Ladies', built between the 1870s and 1906, drip with rich exterior decoration, strong architectural lines and bright colours. About 13,000 Victorian buildings survive, most of them in the Castro, Haight-Ashbury, Pacific Heights and Fillmore districts. **Victorian Home Walk** (*tel: 415-252-9485; $*) offers an easy walking introduction to the architecture.

Yerba Buena Gardens

Between 4th, Mission, 3rd and Howard Sts.

The former slum is a shopping, entertainment and arts centre built atop underground Moscone Convention Center. 'Gardens' applies only to the actual public garden in the centre of the development. **Zeum** is a high-tech, high-touch arts centre with an ice-skating rink, bowling centre and restored carousel. **Metreon** includes an IMAX cinema, 15-screen cineplex, interactive play areas based on children's books, restaurants and famous-name retail shopping. In **Ansel Adams Center for Photography** rotating exhibits of Adams photographs lure visitors into other galleries (*250 4th St; tel: 415-495-7000; open daily 1100–1700; $*). The **Cartoon Art Museum** has comic books, editorial cartoons, animation cells and advertisements (*814 Mission St, 2nd floor; tel: 415-227-8666; open Wed–Sun; $*). **San Francisco Museum of Modern Art (SFMOMA)** is known for Mario Botta's distinctive architectural design and Northern California's largest collection of modern art (*151 Third St; tel: 415-357-4000; web: www.sfmoma.org; open Fri–Tue 1100–1800, Thur to 2100 (1800–2100 half-price), free first Tue each month; $$*). The **Mexican Museum** and the **Jewish Museum** plan to join Yerba Buena's museum row.

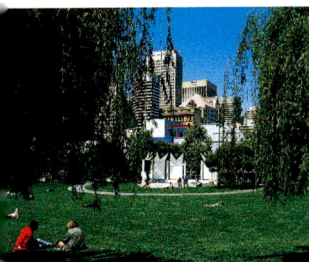

Eating out in San Francisco

Food is more religion than sustenance in San Francisco. The city claims more restaurants (and bars) per capita than any other city in America – more than 3000 – but few survive the fierce competition for more than a few months.

The *San Francisco Bay Guardian* has a good selection of current reviews, but with chefs changing more often than table linens, a kitchen that was outstanding last week could be mediocre tomorrow. The most reliable guide is the *Zagat Survey: San Francisco Bay Area Restaurants,* available at booksellers.

Aqua

252 California St. Tel: 415-956-9662. $$$. Rich and elegant natural wood and simple décor only emphasise the best fish in town.

BIX

56 Gold St. Tel: 415-433-6300. $$$. A jazzy, sophisticated, two-level supper club with the whiff of a martini in the Financial District.

Boudin Sourdough Bakery & Café

156 Jefferson (and other locations). Tel: 415-928-1849. $. Fisherman's Wharf's best sandwiches and clam chowder in a sourdough loaf bowl are a tasty antidote to fast food.

Boulevard

1 Mission St. Tel: 415-543-6084. $$$. Beaux Arts décor and succulent French-inspired dishes offset indifferent service near the Ferry Building and the Embarcadero.

Buena Vista Café

2765 Hyde St. Tel: 415-474-5044. $$$. Irish whiskey and whipped cream is still a best-seller where the concoction was created in 1952, across from the Cable Car turnaround.

Fior d'Italia

601 Union St. Tel: 415-986-1886. $$$. America's oldest surviving Italian restaurant (1886) is also one of the most gracious, across from the heart of North Beach, Washington Square.

Golden Spike

527 Columbus Ave. Tel: 415-421-4591. $$. Minestrone soup and gargantuan portions of North Beach antipasto, pasta and main dishes are staples at this casual family-style eatery.

Masa's

648 Bush St in Hotel Vintage Court. Tel: 415-989-7154. $$$. For years, through several chefs, this dining spot has always got rave reviews for the finest French cuisine matched by exquisite service.

McCormick & Kuleto's Seafood Restaurant

900 North Point, Ghirardelli Square. Tel: 415-929-1730. $$$. Huge view windows, a well-stocked bar and good appetisers and entrées match the views of San Francisco Bay.

Garden Court

Sheraton Palace Hotel, Market and New Montgomery Sts. Tel: 415-512-1111. $$$. Dine under the Kew Gardens Conservatory-style dome amidst palms, take tea in the afternoon or listen to a romantic pianist in the evening.

Park Grill

333 Battery St, Park Hyatt Hotel. Tel: 415-296-2933. $$$. Great service in a Financial District business hotel. The grill has great food, too, from innovative fresh salads and the grills themselves to dessert and coffee.

Plumpjack Café

3127 Fillmore St. Tel: 415-563-4755. $$$. Scions of wealthy San Francisco families took the name from Sir John Falstaff and added a passion for wine and fine dining to the concept.

Postrio

545 Post St, Prescott Hotel. Tel: 415-776-7825. $$$. Celebrity chef Wolfgang Puck's little goat-cheese pizzas are still delicious at this light, airy restaurant near Union Square.

Ritz-Carlton Terrace

600 Stockton St, Ritz-Carlton Hotel. Tel: 415-296-7465. $$$. Inside or outside, the Sunday Brunch, with a jazz combo in late spring–summer, is the best San Francisco has to offer.

Rubicon

558 Sacramento St. Tel: 415-434-4100. $$$. Actors Robin Williams and Robert De Niro, and director Francis Ford Coppola own a piece of the fine dining action at this Financial District hot spot.

Twenty Tank Brewery

316 11th St. Tel: 415-255-9455. $. Basic working-class and the city's best brewery-restaurant. A convenient spot to start before a night of SOMA clubbing.

Shopping

There's no shortage of places to exercise your credit cards or window shop. Retro-hipsters head for **Haight St. Union Square** sports the most expensive marquees, from Disney and Nike to Saks Fifth Avenue and Tiffany. **Union Street** caters to the stylishly trendy, pricey shops in elegant Victorian buildings offering bric-à-brac from around the world. T-shirts and souvenirs are abundant along Fisherman's Wharf, where **Ghirardelli Square** (*900 North Point; tel: 415-775-5500*), **The Cannery** (*2801 Leavenworth St; tel: 415-771-3112*) and **Pier 39** (*the Embarcadero*) have more original shops. A former bayside chocolate factory in Ghirardelli Square is a bustling retail/shopping/entertainment complex – the hot fudge sundaes at **Swenson's Ice Cream Parlor** (*tel: 415-399-9415; $$*) are superb. San Francisco Sourdough French Bread, doughy and sour, is a take-home tradition, widely available at supermarkets and the SFO (airport).

49

Frisky, not 'Frisco

San Francisco has been serious about fun since the days when Gold Rush miners tossed bouquets of roses to touring opera stars and pouches of gold dust to bouncing dance-hall girls. City stages and concert halls offer the range from Punk to Pavarotti all neatly indexed in the pink Datebook Section *in the* San Francisco Sunday Chronicle *newspaper. The free, widely available* SF Bay Guardian *and* SF Weekly *concentrate on more avant-garde offerings and club listings.*

The Barbary Coast 'anything goes' attitude survives, despite one of the nation's highest costs of living and the need to support an indulgent lifestyle. The tolerance extends to some of the more unusual restaurants and entertainment spots found anywhere.

SOMA

Between Market St, The Embarcadero, Townsend, Division and 12th Sts.

The hottest entertainment scene is in **SOMA**, shorthand for the South of Market Area. The former industrial district filled with brick buildings and dark alleyways has metamorphosed into a trendy residential and entertainment neighbourhood. Clubs suit every taste in music, dress, sex and drugs. Check the *SF Bay Guardian* and *SF Weekly* newspapers for current acts.

At **AsiaSF** (*201 9th St; tel: 415-255-2742; $$*) 'boy illusionists', beautifully made up as ladies, serve dinner and entertain in drag. **The Endup** (*401 6th St at Harrison St;*

tel: 415-357-0827; open Wed–Mon, hours vary beyond 2200–0400) varies the programme nightly, from Sun afternoon tea dances to 'Fag Fridays' to leather and studs, beneath the building's changing wall murals, once the sun goes down. Darkness is SOMA's witching hour, late evening when the mostly young, studded and pierced crowd drinks, parties and indulges. **Entros** (270 Brannan at 2nd Sts; tel: 415-495-5150; open Tue–Sun 1730–0200; $$$) serves good Asian cuisine with Southwest touches, but dinner is a game, literally. Waiters are guides to computer and other games such as 'Time Portal', which seldom lets diners *sit* because they have to search for clues stashed all over the eatery.

Soul training

The **Audium** (1616 Bush St; tel: 415-771-1616) is 1960s music meets Millennium meditation, with speakers mixing thousands of sounds in a continuous flow of music – in total darkness. Walking meditation, *sans* shoes, is the drill at the (Episcopal) **Grace Cathedral Labyrinth** (1100 California St, Nob Hill; tel: 415-749-6300), a copy of the famed 12th-century maze in France's Chartres Cathedral. Music with salvation, saxophones, a choir and breathtaking Russian-style painted icons of seminal jazz saxophonist John Coltrane and other notables creates Sunday noontime joy at the iconoclastic African Orthodox **Church of Saint John Coltrane** (351 Divisadero at Oak Sts; tel: 415-621-4054. Sun at 1145).

Giggles and thrills

Beach Blanket Babylon (678 Beach St; tel: 415-421-4222; $$) is a spoof of popular American culture from a (skewed) San Francisco perspective. Running for a quarter-century, the show's songs, scripts, characters and hats are updated regularly to reflect current events and politic(ian)s. Depending on the programme, you may be alone or sitting with 50 others in the intimate armchair atmosphere of an independent film/art film cinema, **The Casting Couch** (950 Battery St; tel: 415-986-7001) with ale and brews served seatside. **Tix** (Union Square; tel: 415-433-7827) sells half-price tickets for mainstream theatre, dance and music events on performance day, cash only. Credit cards are accepted for full-price advance tickets.

Mellow
Marin

Marin. It's the most accessible coastal countryside in Northern California. The real-life possibilities sound like a make-believe travel catalogue: fine beaches and booming surf, virgin redwood groves, sunny grasslands, sheer cliffs, windy picnics and elegant hideaways. The potential for outdoor recreation isn't lost on Marinites, who crowd their communal back yard every weekend.

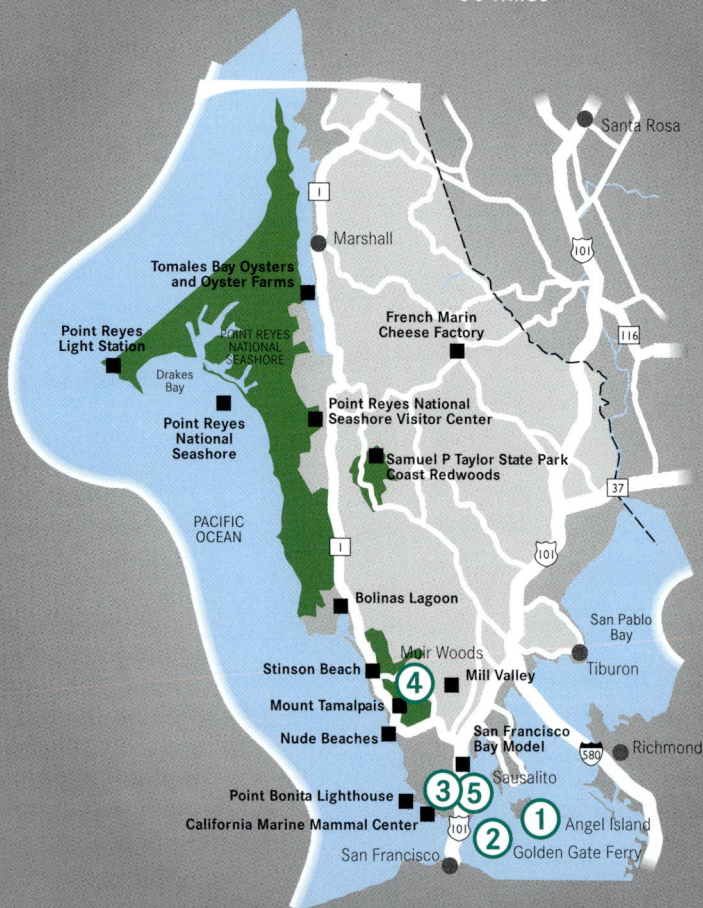

BEST OF
Mellow Marin

North
↑

0 ___ 100 kms
0 ___ 50 miles

Santa Rosa

1

Marshall

Tomales Bay Oysters
and Oyster Farms

French Marin
Cheese Factory

116

Point Reyes
Light Station

POINT REYES
NATIONAL
SEASHORE

Drakes
Bay

Point Reyes National
Seashore Visitor Center

Point Reyes
National
Seashore

Samuel P Taylor State Park
Coast Redwoods

37

PACIFIC
OCEAN

101

Bolinas Lagoon

San Pablo
Bay

Muir Woods

Stinson Beach

Mill Valley

Tiburon

4

Mount Tamalpais

Nude Beaches

San Francisco
Bay Model

Richmond

580

Sausalito

Point Bonita Lighthouse

3 5

California Marine Mammal Center

1 Angel Island

101

2

San Francisco

Golden Gate Ferry

MELLOW MARIN

① Angel Island State Park

Millions see the largest island in San Francisco Bay every day, but almost nobody has actually set foot on its rolling hillsides. Their loss. **Page 56**

② Ferry service

It's easy enough to drive to Marin from San Francisco, but a ferry is the only civilised way to travel – and the most scenic. **Page 59**

③ Marin Headlands

Ever wondered what San Francisco looked like before San Francisco was there? A lot like the Marin Headlands, the bare, wind-whipped hills directly north of the Golden Gate Bridge. **Pages 60–61**

④ Muir Woods National Monument

This pocket-sized forest is a delight to explore, a calm and majestic grove of virgin coastal redwoods tucked into the folds of Mount Tamalpais, the largest mountain in Marin County. **Page 62**

⑤ Sausalito

The town that once elected one of San Francisco's most successful bordello owners as mayor can't be all boring. **Page 63**

Getting there:

Most visitors drive (or walk or cycle) over the Golden Gate Bridge from San Francisco. It's also possible to take a bus or ferry, although using public transport does limit your options once you've arrived (*Ferry service, page 59*).

Back to the Future

The Marin County Civic Center, just south of San Rafael on Hwy 101, was the last building designed by famed American architect Frank Lloyd Wright. The futuristic building with the golden spire tower (a disguised smokestack) still stars in sci-fi epics a quarter-century after it opened, but the roof leaks.

Angel Island State Park

San Francisco Bay. Tel: 415-435-1915; web: www.cal-parks.ca.gov/DISTRICTS/marin/aisp231.htm. Open daily. Admission: $.

Angel Island is one of Marin's most splendid – and least appreciated – natural wonders. Beaches, ridges, grasslands, forested slopes and 13 miles of hiking trails are open all year. Bicycles can be hired (*daily May–Sept, Wed–Sun Apr, Oct; weekends only Mar, Nov*). If cycling seems too vigorous, a motorised tram circles the island every hour with an audio history tour, **Angel Island Company** (*tel: 415-897-0715; $*). Picnic spots circle the island like a compass, or check into the **Cove Café** (*next to the ferry landing at Ayala Cove; $*) during the summer months.

Sea kayak tours circumnavigate Angel Island from March to November (**Sea Trek**: *tel: 415-488-1000; $$*) with the emphasis on natural history and ecology. By turns, this rolling 750-acre island has been a rich hunting and fishing ground for Coastal Miwok Indians, a haven for Spanish explorers, cattle ranch, US Army post, America's main port of entry for immigrants from Asia, prisoner of war camp, Nike missile base and State Park. The only access is by boat, but **Blue & Gold Fleet** (*tel: 415-435-1915*) ferries serve the island from San Francisco, Sausalito or Tiburon. Blue & Gold also sells combination tours that visit Angel Island and **Alcatraz** (*see page 40*) in a single day.

Bodega Bay

Bodega Bay Chamber of Commerce, 575 Hwy 1. Tel: 707-875-3422 or 800-905-9050. Open Mon–Fri 0900–1700.

Alfred Hitchcock pictured Bodega Bay as a town under siege from the air in *The Birds*, his 1963 film that pitted sea gulls, crows and sparrows against the human population – the birds won. Birds still flock to the harbour, but they're more interested in cadging for scraps than in chasing tourists or school children. The Potter Schoolhouse Hitchcock used to horrific effect is still here, east from the harbour on Bay Hwy.

Unsinkable ferries

The 1938 erection of the Golden Gate Bridge had killed ferry traffic between Marin and San Francisco by the 1950s, but popular demand – and burgeoning bridge traffic – brought the ferries back onto San Francisco Bay in 1970.

Hitchcock and Hollywood boosted Bodega's economy, but the town fell into dire straits as commercial fishing declined in the 1970s. Fortunately, holiday-makers discovered Bodega's pleasant harbourfront and expansive, largely undeveloped coastline. The beaches are too windy and the water too cold (and rough) for swimming. Across the bay, cycle or walk on **Bodega Head**. Look for the 'hole in the head', a vast pit once slotted as the site of a nuclear power station. Local residents successfully rallied against the building of a reactor directly atop the San Andreas earthquake fault. The **University of California Bodega Bay Marine Station** (*Westside Rd, Bodega Head; tel: 707-875-2211; open Fri 1400–1600; free*) displays local marine creatures with research programmes. Don't miss the bright blue lobsters.

Bolinas

Unmarked paved road turning from Hwy 1 beyond Bolinas Lagoon.

Anybody who manages to find their way to this enclave of greying and balding counter-culture survivors is welcome, if only because visitors are in relatively short supply. Thank (or blame) the Bolinas Brigade, an informal group dedicated to preserving their isolation and paucity of tourists by uprooting highway direction signs. Stop at the ***People's Store*** for picnic supplies, local produce and helpful service. *End of the gravel drive, next to Bolinas Bakery. Tel: 415-868-1433. $.*

Bolinas Lagoon

Just N of Stinson Beach off Hwy 1.

Marin is replete with natural areas of unnatural allure. The shallow lagoon is usually sunny and usually filled with seabirds and harbour seals which haul out on sandbars. Off the eastern side of the Lagoon is **Audubon Canyon Ranch Bolinas Lagoon Preserve** (*tel: 415-868-9244; free, donations accepted*), the best place along the West Coast of North America to observe majestic great blue herons as well as dozens of other species. Hike up the canyon walls to peer *down* into nests set in the crowns of redwoods and gum trees.

California Marine Mammal Center

Marin Headlands. Tel: 415-331-7325. Open daily. Admission: free.

California's oldest and most successful hospital and rehabilitation centre for marine mammals usually treats seals and sea lions, but staff see the occasional whale. The centre is open for tours – volunteer staff and workload permitting.

Duxbury Reef Nature Reserve

End of Elm Rd, Bolinas. Open daily.

Duxbury is the mother of all tidepools, a broad, rocky shelf pock-marked with pools from hand size to swimming pools. Watch ocean waves, especially on a rising tide. Another favourite with weekend warriors is **Point Reyes Bird Observatory** (*Mesa Rd; tel: 415-868-1221; open daily*). The visitor centre and nature trail are self-guiding.

Ferry service

A ferry is the easiest, most scenic and most relaxed way to travel between San Francisco and Marin. Marinites crowd commuter ferries Monday to Friday, but even the most crowded run offers ample space to soak up sun and views without worrying about traffic clogging the Golden Gate Bridge high above the Bay. Weekend ferries are even less crowded. The **Blue & Gold Fleet** (*tel: 415-435-1915*) serves Sausalito, Tiburon, Alcatraz and Angel Island from the Pier 41 area in San Francisco; **Golden Gate Ferry** (*tel: 415-923-2000*) sails between Sausalito and Tiburon and the Ferry Building, at the foot of Market St in San Francisco.

Marin French Cheese Factory

2500 Red Hill Rd, Petaluma. Tel: 707-762-6001; web: www.sfnet.net/cheesefactory. Open daily 0900–1700, tours 1000–1600.

This family-owned factory is one of the most successful cheese-making operations in Northern California, right down to the racks of cheese rounds growing carefully cultivated coats of mould as they age. Specialities are local versions of Brie, Camembert (French) and Schlosskaese (Austrian), all of them tasting more authentic than the processed, plastic imports that usually reach US supermarkets. Factory tours and picnicking around a peaceful lake are free; the cheese is reasonably priced.

How green are my hills

Eighty per cent of Marin County is open space, nearly all of it protected by an interlocking network of federal, state and local landholdings and agricultural preserves.

Marin Headlands

Golden Gate National Recreation Area headquarters on MacArthur St, upper Fort Mason, San Francisco. Tel: 415-56-0560; web: www.nps.gov/goga. Marin Headlands Visitor Information Center: tel: 415-331-1540. Open daily 0930–1630.

The Headlands won't win any urban planning prizes, but the nearly naked hillsides are the most natural scenery within sight of San Francisco Bay and a popular recreation area – thanks to the US Army.

During World War II, slopes facing the Pacific Ocean and the Golden Gate were honeycombed with artillery emplacements, observation posts and supply bunkers, but the natural surface terrain and vegetation were retained as camouflage. Anti-aircraft batteries and Nike missile launchers were added during the Cold War years, but military planners never envisaged any large-scale use for the Headlands – they much preferred the Presidio on the south side of the Golden Gate, similar terrain that had been planted with cedar and pine forests, rolling lawns and golf courses. Once intercontinental ballistic missiles had rendered San Francisco's air-defence grid obsolete, the Army began pulling back from Marin and turned the Headlands over to the National Park Service and the **Golden Gate National Recreation Area (GGNRA)**.

Roads through the Headlands are steep, narrow and slow, but the abandoned batteries have stunning viewpoints. One of the best is **Battery**

MELLOW MARIN

Wallace (*above the southwestern tip of the Headlands*), which frames views of the Golden Gate Bridge from the Pacific Ocean side. The last surviving **Nike Missile Site** (*tel: 415-331-1540; open Mon–Fri 1230–1530 and first Sun each month*) displays decommissioned missiles that look like something out of an antique comic book. **Point Bonita Lighthouse** (*western tip of the Headlands*) offers tours (*see page 62*). Most Headlands activities are based at the **Marin Headlands Visitor Center** (*tel: 415-331-1540*) just around the point from the lighthouse access road. A wide, sandy beach blocks the chill Pacific surf from the warmer, shallow waters of **Rodeo Lagoon** (no swimming, to protect nesting birds) and the **Marine Mammal Center** (*see page 58*). The **Fort Barry Youth Hostel** (*bldg 941; tel: 415-331-2777; $*), a popular base for cycle and walking tours, is converted officers' quarters.

Mount Tamalpais

801 Panoramic Hwy. Tel: 415-388-2070. web: www.cal-parks.ca.gov/ DISTRICTS/marin/mtsp239.htm. Open daily 0700–1700. Admission: $.

The bulk of Mount Tamalpais (Mt Tam to locals) looms above Marin and the north end of San Francisco Bay. Most of the park is undeveloped, but more than 50 miles of walking, equestrian and mountain-bike trails wind across the slopes to connect with another 200 miles of trails. Panoramic views from the peak stretch from the Farallon Islands (26 miles west) to the Sierra Nevada (150 miles east), fog permitting – you're likely to see further in winter than in summer, when fog blankets the coast most days. Ridge lines climbing the 2571ft peak conveniently split Marin. The wild, almost-empty western slopes drop into the Pacific Ocean while the eastern flanks are covered with creeping housing estates that overlook San Francisco Bay to the south and east.

> **"** *In all my wanderings, I have never had a more glorious experience!* **"**
>
> **Sir Arthur Conan Doyle, after riding the 281-turn, 8¼ mile railway between the top of Mount Tamalpais and Mill Valley. The railway burned in 1930.**

Muir Woods National Monument

Panoramic Highway. Tel: 415-388-2595; web: www.nps.gov/muwo. Open daily 0800–1700. Admission: $.

Paved trails circle Muir Woods, touched by tatters of fog and beams of sunlight filtering through 250ft-tall coastal redwood trees surrounded by lush ferns and laurels. This 560-acre virgin grove is all that remains on Mount Tamalpais of the vast redwood forests that once cloaked coastal California from Santa Cruz north into Oregon. Crowds are smallest midweek and least in winter, when spawning salmon and steelhead trout migrate up **Redwood Creek**. *Tel: 415-388-2595, Nov–Mar*, for spawning and fish-viewing updates.

Nude beaches

'Clothing optional' beaches aren't exactly legal, nor are they exactly hidden. Police officers generally turn a blind eye to beach-goers who shed bathing costumes at the far end of the beach, though public nudity is illegal. One of the most popular nude beaches is **Red Rock** (*off Hwy 1, 5 miles south of Stinson Beach; web: www.redrockbeach.com*).

Point Bonita Lighthouse

Western tip of Marin Headlands. Tel: 415-331-1540. Call for hours. Free.

Point Bonita, on the northern side of the Golden Gate, is one of Marin's ultimate feel-good treks. A half-mile path leads to hand-hewn tunnels and a swaying footbridge, with San Francisco hovering beyond the mist. Don't pass up an opportunity for a sunset or full-moon tour conducted by GGNRA rangers.

San Francisco Bay – Delta Tidal Hydraulic Model

2100 Bridgeway, Sausalito. Tel: 415-332-3870. Open Tue–Sat 0900–1600. Admission: free.

The Bay Model is perfect for everyone who has always wondered what the Golden Gate looks like under water. That's not why the US Army Corps of Engineers built the Model – the mundane purpose is to test the impact of development, reclamation, dredging and pollution control before spoiling the real Bay – but the unseen side of the Golden Gate is a good reason to duck inside the ageing warehouse on the Sausalito waterfront.

Sausalito

Sausalito Chamber of Commerce, Village Fair Center, 777 Bridgeway. Tel: 415-332-0505. Open Tue–Sun 1130–1600.

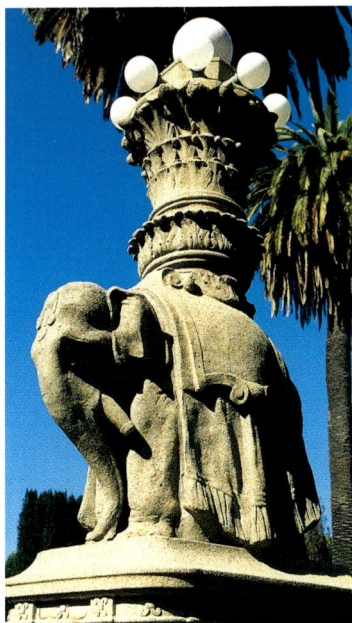

To see the waterfront is to see Sausalito. The best views are from a San Francisco ferry or a 3-hour guided sea-kayak tour from **Sea Trek Ocean Kayaking Center** (*tel: 415-488-1000; fare: $$*).

A National Historic Landmark District protects most of the town centre, including the Spanish-style fountain and elephants from the 1915 Panama-Pacific Exposition that grace the **Plaza de Viña del Mar**. For Sausalito's best bay views, walk south along Bridgeway from the Plaza to Second St, Alexander Ave and Fort Baker Rd. The 2-mile trek leads to the child-orientated **Bay Area Discovery Museum** (*557 McReynolds Rd; tel: 415-487-4398; open daily; admission: $*), but the real draw is the massive bulk of the Golden Gate Bridge looming high above.

Eating out in West Marin

Habitués call it 'Marvellous Marin' or 'God's Country'. Both names reflect the easy-going style of living that has become the goal of life north of the Golden Gate Bridge, if not always the reality. Marinites work just as long and just as hard as their more urban colleagues, but they also play hard – and expect all the conveniences of modern civilisation close at hand. Fine food has become the norm, even in the relative wilds of West Marin.

Bodega Bay

Breakers Café

1400 Hwy 1. Tel: 707-875-2513. $$. Ranks as one of the top choices for nouvelle California seafood.

Lucas Wharf Restaurant

595 Hwy 1. Tel: 707-875-3522; web: www.lucaswharf.com. $$. Lucas serves more traditional seafood; next door, at **Lucas Wharf Deli and Fishmarket** (*$*), pick up a picnic lunch to take to the beach.

Marshall

Tony's Seafood Restaurant

18863 Hwy 1. Tel: 415-663-1107. $$. Locals have been feasting on oysters, crab and other local seafood at Tony's for half a century.

Muir Beach

The Pelican Inn

Hwy 1. Tel: 415-383-6000. $$. This inviting 16th-century Tudor Inn was built in the 20th century by a homesick British expatriate. Sir Francis Drake might not recognise the California *nouvelle* version of shepherd's pie, but legions of the Marin faithful do, in a dining-room rich with dark wood panelling and fireside atmosphere.

Point Reyes Station

Bovine Bakery

Main St. Tel: 415-663-9420. $. The cows produce warm muffins and pastries – mostly organic.

Point Reyes Roadhouse & Oyster Bar

10905 Hwy 1. Tel: 415-663-1277. $$.
The Roadhouse serves the best local selection of microbrews and North Coast wines. It's also a good oyster stop if you don't want to drive the rest of the way to Tomales Bay.

Station House Café

11180 Hwy 1 (Main St). Tel: 415-663-1515. $$. This local favourite for grilled seafood and steaks is packed for breakfast, lunch or dinner.

Taqueria La Quinta

11285 Hwy 1. Tel: 415-663-8868. $. This taqueria is the best Mexican eatery in coastal Marin – and maybe the only one.

Stinson Beach

The Parkside Café

43 Arenal Ave. Tel: 415-868-1272. $$. Take an outdoor table when the weather permits. But even the indoor seating is popular for breakfast and lunch. Dinner is more expensive, but equally busy.

Stinson Beach Grill

3465 Hwy 1. Tel: 415-868-2002. $$. This informal grill dishes up even hamburgers with panache and flourishes.

Shopping

Tomales Bay Oysters

Tomales Bay is a born-again oyster farm that ships its bivalves up and down the Pacific Coast. The **Tomales Bay Oyster Company** has oysters by the bag, by the jar, whole, shucked or any other way you want them – except cooked (*15479 Hwy 1, just S of Marshall; tel: 415-663-1242; open daily 0900–1700; $$*).

Private pleasures

Lucas Valley Rd, which runs west from Hwy 101 through rolling hills in central Marin, was on the maps long before Star Wars *director George Lucas turned his Skywalker Ranch into one of the world's highest-tech cinema studios, including Industrial Light & Magic. Unexpected visitors are* not *welcome.*

Point Reyes National Seashore

Point Reyes Station. Tel: 415-663-1092; web: www.nps.gov/pore. Open daily. Admission: free.

Point Reyes is a busy patch of semi-wilderness surrounded by the Pacific Ocean and Tomales Bay. This wing-shaped peninsula of rolling hills, sheer cliffs and drifting fog is a mecca for hikers, cyclists, backpackers, mountain bikers, sea kayakers, wildflower enthusiasts, birdwatchers and just about anyone else who enjoys outdoor activities.

Bear Valley is the heart of Point Reyes. The unpainted visitor centre, designed to resemble the enormous dairy barns that once dotted Point Reyes, holds exhibits on local ecosystems and a large selection of books on the region. Directly behind the centre stands a real barn, the **Morgan Horse Ranch**, for the working horses rangers ride to patrol the vast wilderness and seashore areas. An easy half-mile trail leads to **Kule Loklo**, a recreated slice of Coastal Miwok village life before the first Europeans arrived (*Bear Valley Visitor Center, Bear Valley, off Hwy 1 from Olema; tel: 415-663-1092; open Mon–Fri 0900–1700, Sat–Sun 0800–1700*).

The **Earthquake Trail** is a flat, mile-long loop trail that shows off some of the few visible scars from the 1906 earthquake that devastated San Francisco. The quake was even more powerful at Point Reyes, where fences and highways that crossed the San Andreas Fault were ripped apart. Another popular hike follows an easy 8-mile return path over rolling hills to the coast at **Arch Rock**. Ask rangers about conditions before you set out. Bear Valley is often a warm, protected pocket of sunshine when the coast is cold, wet and blustery.

MELLOW MARIN

Drakes Beach (*off Sir Francis Drake Blvd*), a calm strand nestled against white sandstone cliffs behind the crook of Point Reyes, is named after English adventurer Sir Francis Drake. The beach and its shallow estuary (**Drakes Estero**) are thought to be where Drake spent five weeks repairing his vessel, the *Golden Hinde*, 1579. **Great Beach** (*off Sir Francis Drake Blvd*) is often called Point Reyes Beach. High surf and strong currents make swimming dangerous, but the wave action is awe-inspiring. Winter waves toss tree trunks about like ragged toothpicks. **Limantur Beach** (*end of Limantur Rd*), sheltered by the Point Reyes Headland, is one of the better swimming beaches in the area. The water is cold but the beach is seldom crowded.

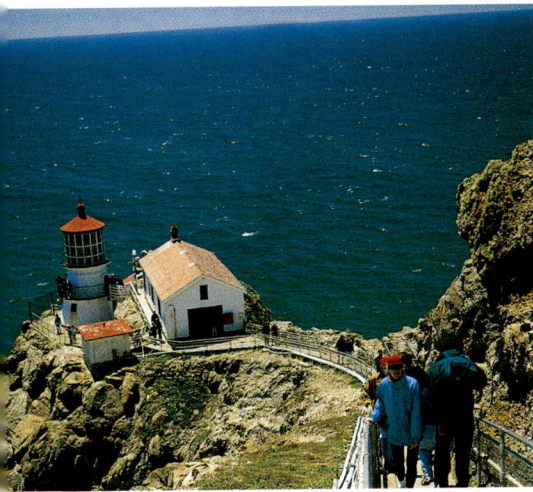

The wind-whipped red-roof **Point Reyes Light Station** is at the tip of Point Reyes, 300 steps down from the Visitor Center. Views from both the centre and the lighthouse are stunning, but dress warmly. The wind can be bitingly cold, even on sunny days (*End of Sir Francis Drake Blvd; tel: 415-669-1534; Visitor Center open Thur–Mon 1000–1700; Lighthouse stairs and exhibits open to 1630; lens room open as staffing permits*).

The day the earth moved

The tiny hamlet of Olema (pop 125), at the south end of Tomales Bay, was the epicentre of the 1906 earthquake that levelled much of San Francisco. The San Andreas Fault caused the Point Reyes Peninsula to jump 16ft north, leaving fissures in the land still visible today.

Northern California Wine Country

The race is on. For sheer numbers of medals won at wine competitions, Napa Valley versus Sonoma County is a dead heat. For appellations and varieties of wine-making styles, sheer size and variety of geography give Sonoma County the edge. But when it comes to name recognition, Napa rules. Decades of dedicated promotion have turned the narrow, 30-mile corridor into a Wine Country theme park, complete with adoring crowds during the summer and every weekend.

AINE ⋆ C

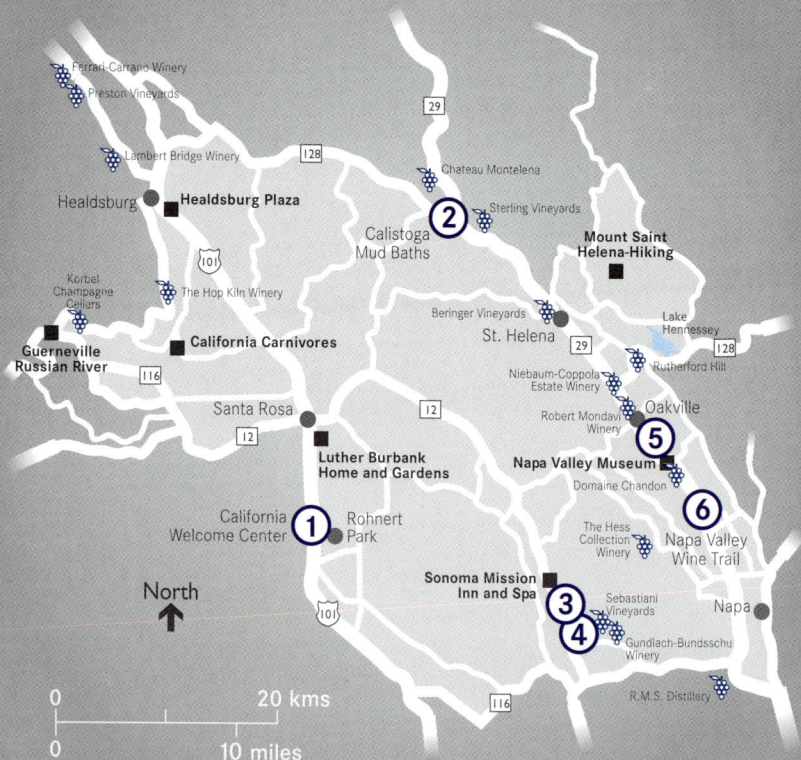

BEST OF
Northern California Wine Country

Ferrari-Carano Winery
Preston Vineyards
Lambert Bridge Winery

128

29

Chateau Montelena

Sterling Vineyards

②

Healdsburg   Healdsburg Plaza

Calistoga
Mud Baths

Mount Saint
Helena-Hiking

Korbel
Champagne
Cellars

101

The Hop Kiln Winery

Beringer Vineyards

St. Helena

29

Lake
Hennessey

Guerneville
Russian River

116

California Carnivores

Niebaum-Coppola
Estate Winery

Rutherford Hill

128

Santa Rosa

12

12

Robert Mondavi
Winery

Oakville

⑤

Luther Burbank
Home and Gardens

Napa Valley Museum

Domaine Chandon

California
Welcome Center

①

Rohnert
Park

The Hess
Collection
Winery

Napa Valley
Wine Trail

⑥

North

101

Sonoma Mission
Inn and Spa

③

Sebastiani
Vineyards

④

Napa

Gundlach-Bundschu
Winery

116

R.M.S. Distillery

0   20 kms

0   10 miles

NORTHERN CALIFORNIA WINE COUNTRY

① California Welcome Center

This is the most complete visitor information centre in Wine Country, right down to tasting, bottle sales and touring information. **Below**

② Calistoga mud baths

Mud bath isn't an oxymoron, at least not to spa-lovers who swear by hot mud as the ultimate way to get clean. Check it out in Calistoga, where geothermal springs, volcanic mud and a relaxed atmosphere have come together in California's most relaxed spa town. **Page 72**

③ Hot-air ballooning

Leave your alarm clock at home. The standard Wine Country wake-up call is the pre-dawn roar of blowtorches from hot-air balloons drifting low above the vineyards. **Page 74**

④ Sonoma Plaza

The town of Sonoma has survived half a century of gentrification with much of its original country allure intact. Thank Gen Mariano Vallejo and the 8-acre plaza he laid out in 1835. **Page 75**

⑤ A question of taste

Decide for yourself which is the best among the vineyards in the area. We've listed only a selection! **Pages 76–79**

⑥ Napa Valley Wine Train

The train is the easiest way to see the famous wineries that line Hwy 29 along the western side of the Napa Valley. See is the operative word – the train doesn't stop for winery tours. **Page 78**

Getting there

The Napa Valley is located due north and a little west of San Francisco Bay. Hwy 29 is the main traffic artery, running up the west side of the Valley. Silverado Trail, along the east side of the Valley, is usually less crowded and more scenic, but slower to drive. Sonoma County's various wine areas surround Hwy 101 north of Marin County.

71

Tourist information

California Welcome Center *5000 Roberts Lake Rd, Rohnert Park. Tel: 707-586-3795; web: www.sonomawine.com. Open daily.* You can get information, if not objectivity, at this best visitor information centre in Wine Country. Staff happily answer questions about Napa, but they know there's a reason that old-timers call Sonoma 'The Ultimate'.

Calistoga mud baths

What began as a string of therapeutic mud baths has grown into one of California's favourite spa resort areas. Treatments range from straightforward soaks in unadulterated mineral water to near-baptism in dense volcanic mud, grape-and-herbal wraps and deep tissue torture, better known as massage. As a general rule, the more expensive the spa, the more exotic the treatment. Down-to-earth spas line Lincoln Ave, where a full mineral bath, blanket wrap, steam bath and massage cost less than a single treatment at one of the town's upmarket retreats.

Dr Wilkinson's Hot Springs (*1507 Lincoln Ave; tel: 707-942-4102; $$$*) caters for the rich, the famous and film stars wanting privacy. **Lavender Hill Spa** (*1015 Foothill Blvd; tel: 707-942-4495; $$$*) uses goo made of ocean kelp to thin its mud (a heavy mixture of volcanic ash and mineral-rich water at most spas).

The same Calistoga mineral water used in mud baths and bottled Calistoga drinking water bubbles to the surface at **Old Faithful Geyser** (*1299 Tubbs Ln; tel: 707-942-6463; web: www.oldfaithfulgeyser.com; open 0900–1600 in winter, to 1700 in summer; $*). Old Faithful was born when an exploratory oil rig tapped into a geothermal vein in the 1920s. Landowners eventually gave up on capping the irrepressible geyser's boiling water and steam and turned its regular half-hourly eruptions into predictable cash. Volcanic **Mount St Helena** (4344ft) erupted 3 million years ago, left traces like Old Faithful and transformed a dense redwood forest into the stony **Petrified Forest**. (*4100 Petrified Forest Rd (5 miles west); tel: 707-942-6667; web: www.petrifiedforest.org; open Wed–Sun 1000–1630 in winter, daily 1000–1800 in summer; admission: $*).

Guerneville

Not invented here

The first grapes in California were planted by Fra Junipero Serra at Mission San Diego about 1769. Jean Louis Vines planted the state's first recorded commercial vineyard in what is now downtown Los Angeles in the 1820s. Anaheim, famous for orange groves and Disneyland, began as an agricultural settlement for immigrant German grape growers.

There are two reasons to visit Guerneville (pronounced *gurnvil*): wine touring and lazing about the Russian River. This Russian River hamlet began as a logging camp, evolved into a summer resort for beach and redwoods-loving San Franciscans, then drifted into happy obscurity during the hippie era. Modern urban escapees are a mix of hippie-era survivors, sophisticated city-dwellers and gay/lesbian holiday makers.

The Russian River often floods during the winter rainy season, but in summer, **Johnson's Beach**, in the centre of town, offers sand, swimming, canoes, rubber rafts and paddle-boats. The beach is also main stage for the wildly popular **Russian River Jazz Festiva**l each September, when every room in the entire Russian River Valley is booked up.

Escape to **Armstrong Redwoods State Reserve**, 750 acres of coastal redwoods (*Armstrong Woods Rd, 2 miles north; tel: 707-869-2015; open 0800–one hour after sunset; admission: $*). Hikers are tempted to strike out across country, but try not to stray off the marked trails; it's easy to get lost in the tangled thickets that fill most of the park. **Armstrong Woods Pack Station** (*tel: 707-887-2939*) offers horse-riding expeditions through the towering groves.

Hess Collection

4411 Redwood Rd, Napa. Tel: 707-255-1144. Open daily.

Hess is as popular for its upstairs collection of outstanding modern art (**Robert Motherwell, Frank Stella**) as for the wines produced below in its stone turn-of-the-century winery, an operation once run by the Christian Brothers order.

Hot-air ballooning

Late risers miss out on one of Wine Country's top thrills: floating above the vineyards just as the dawn mists burn away to reveal long rows of trellised vines sweeping across valleys and up hillsides. Plan on landing 90 minutes later to a sparkling wine breakfast (California vintners can't call their bubbly 'Champagne' if it's going to Europe).

Ballooning is an expensive thrill but worth every penny. Experienced operators include: **Balloons Above the Valley** (*tel: 707-253-2222 or 800-464-2724; web: www.balloonrides.com*); **Napa Valley Balloons** (*tel: 707-253-2224 or 800-253-2224*); **Sonoma Thunder** (t*el: 707-538-7359 or 800-759-5638; web: www.balloontours.com*).

Luther Burbank Gardens

Santa Rosa and Sonoma Aves, Santa Rosa. Tel: 707-524-5445. Open daily. Admission: gardens free, house $.

This square city block is to garden-lovers what the Vatican is to Roman Catholics. The white-framed residence and carefully tended experimental gardens were home to Luther Burbank, a legendary horticulturist who created more than 800 new commercial varieties of fruits, flowers, vegetables and other plants about 100 years ago.

Mount St Helena

The bald crown of Mount St Helena's ancient volcano (4344ft) is probably the hottest, sweatiest and dustiest corner of Wine Country in summer. It's also the top of the wine world, with views that occasionally stretch 200 miles north. Most of the mountain lies within **Robert Louis Stevenson State Park** (*tel: 707-942-4575*), named after the author who, in 1880, honeymooned in an abandoned miner's cabin on the mountainside. His adventure became *Silverado Squatters*. The cabin is long gone, but a plaque marks the site on the $2^1/_2$-mile trail to the summit. Stevenson proclaimed the joys of sampling 18 different sparkling wines from **Schramsberg Vineyards** (*1400 Schramsberg Rd, Calistoga; tel: 707-942-4558*) in a single sitting. Schramsberg is still one of America's better bubblies.

Rutherford Hill

200 Rutherford Hill Rd, Rutherford. Tel: 707-963-7194; web: www.rutherfordhill.com. Open daily 1000–1700.

Rutherford Hill has the best cave tour on the quieter east side of the Napa Valley. The winery's shady picnic ground has expansive views across olive groves, vineyards and the Napa Valley – for free.

Sonoma Plaza

Spain, W First, Napa and E First Sts, Sonoma.

A dozen original adobe buildings still surround the 1835 plaza, including **Mission San Francisco Solano de Sonoma**, **Gen Vallejo's home** and the **Sonoma Barracks**, the **Sonoma State Historic Park** (*20 E Spain St; tel: 707-938-1519; open daily 1000–1700; $*). In this plaza, rebels declared the short-lived Bear Flag Revolt and California Republic in 1846, and imprisoned the town's founder, Gen Vallejo, who favoured annexation by the USA. The 1850 Swiss Hotel (*page 81*) and Sebastiani Sonoma Cask Cellars (*page 79*) are also on the Plaza.

Vineyard selection

Here is a selection of vineyards and wine-related activities in the area. Go to look around and see how and where some of the finest wines are grown and matured (most winery tours are free); to taste (see pages 82–83); or simply to enjoy the scenery.

Beringer Vineyards

2000 Main St, St Helena. Tel: 707-963-7115; web: www.beringer.com. Open daily 0930–1700, tours every half-hour.

Beringer is best known for its wine-ageing caves (tunnels, actually) dug by Chinese and Irish labourers, and the whimsically gothic **Rhine House**. The Napa Valley's most-photographed building was based on an ornate German homestead. Beringer is a regular stop on coach tours: ornate wood panelling, stained-glass windows and a superb Victorian-era tasting room make it worth putting up with the crowds.

Buena Vista Winery

1800 Old Winery Rd, Sonoma. Tel: 707-938-1266. Open daily 1030–1700.

BV, as it is often called, was the first flower of California's modern wine industry, courtesy of Hungarian immigrant **Agoston Haraszthy**, a sometime-Count, sometime-General and full-time schemer. Haraszthy's 1857 vineyards have long since been replanted, but the restored estate, stone winery and hillside tunnels are still open for business. An art gallery and picnic area are somewhat later additions.

Chateau Montelena

1429 Tubbs Ln, Calistoga. Tel: 707-942-5105. Open daily.

Montelena is an only-in-California cultural combination: traditional Italian name, traditional French château façade and equally traditional Chinese garden.

Domaine Chandon

1 California Dr, Yountville. Tel: 707-944-2280; web: www.dchandon.com. Open Wed–Sun 1000–1800 Jan–Mar, daily Apr–Dec.

French Champagne house Moët-Hennessey owns Napa's highest-visibility and busiest sparkling wine maker. The restaurant is posh, tasting is by the glass (*$$*), but the valley's most informative sparkling winery tour is still free.

Ferrari-Carrano Winery

8761 W Dry Creek Rd, Healdsburg. Tel: 707-433-6700. Open daily 1000–1700.

This Italian-style architectural masterpiece produces superb Chardonnay and reds. The owners got their start in the Nevada casino business, but wine seems to be spinning profits as predictably as video poker machines.

Healdsburg Plaza

Healdsburg Ave, Matheson, Center and Plaza Sts, Healdsburg.

This calm plaza is the tree-lined focus for a farming town that still has nearly as many grape growers as tourists – though you'd be hard-pressed to tell one from the other in the summer throngs that flock to Healdsburg's restaurants and boutiques. **The Downtown Bakery & Creamery** (*308A Center St; tel: 707-431-2719; $*) and the **Flying Goat Coffee Roastery and Café** (*324 Center St; tel: 707-433-9081; $*) are favourite early-morning-coffee and gossip stops for locals.

Several wineries have tasting rooms around the plaza, including **Trentadue** (*320 Center St; tel: 707-433-1082; open daily 1000–1700*) and **Windsor** (*308B Center St; tel: 707-433-2822; open Mon–Fri 1000–1700, Sat–Sun 1000–1800*).

Enough wine? Hire a canoe or a rubber raft for a slow afternoon float downstream from **Veterans Memorial Beach** (*Russian River, 1 mile south of the plaza*).

Korbel Champagne Cellars

13250 River Rd, Guerneville. Tel: 707-824-7000. Open 0900–1630 Nov–Mar, 0900–1700 Apr–Oct.

Korbel is a Wine Country giant that makes beer, wine, brandy and Champagne-style sparkling wines. Ivy-cloaked century-old red-brick buildings and gardens planted with 250 varieties of antique roses make its shaded picnic tables one of Sonoma County's most beautiful picnic stops.

Lambert Bridge Winery

4085 W Dry Creek Rd, Healdsburg. Tel: 707-431-9600. Open daily 1030–1630.

Stop at Lambert if you're serious about red wine. Its vineyards are some of the oldest in the area (older means richer flavour, lower production and higher prices) and the cavernous tasting room is light and airy.

Napa Valley Wine Train

1275 McKinstry St, Napa. Tel: 707-253-2111; web: www.winetrain.com. Open daily, departure times vary. Fare: $$, advance bookings essential.

This elegantly restored passenger train makes lunch and dinner runs up and down the Napa Valley. Watch the scenery and the vineyards, but it's still an eat, look and don't stop tour.

Niebaum-Coppola Estate Winery

1991 St Helena Hwy, Rutherford. Tel: 707-963-9099; web: www.niebaum-coppola.com. Open daily 1000–1700.

Niebaum-Coppola is cinema director Francis Ford (*The Godfather*) Coppola's venture into wineland. So far, very good. The historic château has emerged with tasting room intact, cellars enhanced, and Northern California's best cinema memorabilia museum.

Preston Vineyards

9282 W Dry Creek Rd, Healdsburg. Tel: 707-433-3372. Open daily 1100–1630.

Preston seems more like a house than a winery when you first walk in – the seductive odour is fresh-baked bread, not the rich red wines stacked in the cellars. Bread, wine and shaded picnic tables hidden in a flower garden are a heady combination.

Robert Mondavi Winery

7801 St Helena Hwy, Oakville. Tel: 707-226-1335 or 888-766-6328; web: www.robertmondaviwinery.com. Open daily 1000–1600. Book tours a week in advance in summer and at holiday weekends.

Robert Mondavi was America's first superstar winemaker-marketer and the first to turn his winery into a Mission-style architectural ego boost. Tours push the wine, but are a fine introduction to the methodology of wine-making.

Sebastiani Sonoma Cask Cellars

389 Fourth St E, Sonoma. Tel: 707-933-3206; web: www.sebastiani.com. Open daily 1000–1700.

Sebastiani has Sonoma's most informative and light-hearted winery tour. Look for the casks carved with Wine Country motifs and epigrams from family patriarch Samuele Sebastiani, who started with Zinfandel in 1895.

Eating out in Wine Country restaurants

Wine Country is the best place in all of California to shatter budget, diet and cholesterol levels in one mad binge. Since even the most dedicated bingers need to sleep, you might as well have a bed to match your meals.

Auberge du Soleil

180 Rutherford Hill Rd, Rutherford. Tel: 707-963-1211 or 800-348-5406; web: www.aubergedusoleil.com. $$$. With a style imitating Provence, the Mediterranean-inspired inn has valley vistas of olive groves and vineyards.

Bed and Breakfast Inns of Napa Valley

Tel: 707-944-4444. This booking service handles Bed and Breakfasts throughout Wine Country. Expect to pay $$–$$$ anywhere, any season.

Meadowood Resort

900 Meadowood Ln, St Helena. Tel: 707-963-3646 or 800-458-8080; web: www.placestostay.com. $$$. Bungalows are arranged on the slopes amongst the oaks surrounding a private croquet pitch and golf course. Fiercely loyal fans book rooms early.

Back to Wine Country's twin pillars of eating and drinking:

Applewood Inn

13555 Hwy 116, Guerneville. Tel: 707-869-9093 or 800-555-8509; web: www.applewoodinn.com. Open dinner Tue–Sat. $$$. Lovely arbours and a profusion of flowers complement the Russian River's best restaurant and most luxurious inn.

Babette's Restaurant & Wine Bar

464 First St E, Sonoma. Tel: 707-939-8921. Open daily 1200–2200. $$. Sonoma's most popular French restaurant was inspired by the French chef in the film, *Babette's Feast.*

Bistro Ralph

109 Plaza St E, Healdsburg. Tel: 707-433-1380. Open Mon–Fri 1130–1430, daily 1700–late. $$. Ralph is an Italian-California cuisine survivor at the heart of a dedicated restaurant town.

Bosko's Ristorante

1364 Lincoln Ave, Calistoga. Tel: 707-942-9088. Open daily 1100–2200. $$. Italian food never tasted better than at this central restaurant.

La Boucane

1778 Second St, Napa. Tel: 707-253-1177. Open 1730–late. $$$. The best classic French cuisine in Napa.

Brew Moon

16248 Main St, Guerneville. Tel: 707-869-0201. Open 0800–1500. $$. The Russian River's best barbecue joint has Guerneville's best beer selection.

Brix Restaurant & Wine Shop

7377 St Helena Hwy, Yountville. Tel: 707-944-2749. Open daily 1130–1500, 1600–2130. $$$. The name is a measure of wine's sugar content – Brix's California-Italian-French kitchen is one of Napa's best.

Café La Haye

140 E Napa St, Sonoma. Tel: 707-935-5994. Open daily. $$. Dinnertime hops at this American-based café.

Della Santina's

133 E Napa St, Sonoma. Tel: 707-935-0576. Open daily 1100–1500, 1700–2130. $$$. In a town with many Italian restaurants, Della Santina's gets the nod as the best.

Downtown Joe's Restaurant & Brewery

902 Main St, Napa. Tel: 707-258-2337. Open daily 0830–2200. $$. Napa's oldest brewpub serves bistro meals with fresh local ingredients, beers and ales.

Fellion's Delicatessen

1359 Lincoln Ave, Calistoga. Tel: 707 942-6722. Open daily. $. Between mud baths, stock up on picnic supplies.

The French Laundry

6640 Washington St, Yountville. Tel: 707-944-2380. Open 1130–2130. $$$. The Laundry was one of the valley's first big-name eateries and is still one of the most popular.

Madrona Manor

1001 Westside Rd at Dry Creek Rd. Healdsburg. Tel: 707-433-4231 or 800-358-4003; web: www.madronamanor. com. $$$. A formal driveway through a thick tangle of trees, leads to one of the most sought-after restaurants in Healdsburg, revered for ambience, presentation and ingredients fresh from its own exotic gardens.

Mustards Grill

7399 St Helena Hwy, Yountville. Tel: 707-944-2424. Open daily 1130–2100, Fri–Sat to 2200. $$$. Mustards is more California than French and always busy.

Oakville Grocery Co

7865 St Helena Hwy, Oakville. Tel: 707-944-8802. Open daily 0900–1800. There's probably still a roll or two of rusty wire somewhere in the back, but the Napa Valley's oldest farmers' mercantile has become a gourmet haven. The store is packed with food, wine and a lunchtime sandwich queue that sometimes snakes out the door. For a glimpse of Napa before the tourist boom, go into the **Oakville Grocery Café** (*open daily 0500–1500, Thur–Mon 1700–2100; $$; open for $ breakfast around 0600*).

Swiss Hotel

18 W Spain S, Sonoma. Tel: 707-938-2884. Open daily 1130–1430 and 1700–2100. $$. The small 1850 hotel has a stunningly good California cuisine restaurant. Enjoy the period photographs and artefacts on the walls even if you aren't hungry.

Tra Vigna

1050 Charter Oak Ave, St Helena. Tel: 707-963-4444. Open 1130–2200. $$$. Popular, perennially packed, Tra Vigna fans love its California cuisine with an Italian twist.

Wine Spectator Greystone Restaurant

2555 Main St, St Helena. Tel: 707-967-1010. Open 1130–2200. $$$. Greystone is part showcase, part training ground for student chefs from the Culinary Institute of America.

Wine and wine tasting

California wineries have transformed wine tasting into a ritual sacrament and tasting rooms into lavish architectural statements. Traditionally a way to boost bottle sales at the winery, wine tasting is turning into a profitable business all of its own. Expect to pay $2–$5 for tasting at the more popular wineries in Napa, even more to sample sparkling wines. Tasting remains free at most smaller wineries, especially in Sonoma; winery tours are almost always free. Whether paying or sipping for free, wine tasting has more pretension than firm rules. Anyone aged 21 can taste wine in California (children are welcome in tasting rooms, although not at the bar).

Start with white wines, which are generally lighter in taste, then move on to heavier reds and even heavier dessert wines. The idea is to sip the wine, not to swill it – traffic police haunt Wine Country highways in search of drivers who have enjoyed a few too many samples.

Beyond those basics, wine tasting is strictly personal opinion. If a wine doesn't taste good to *you*, ignore what the critics, the winery's own tasting notes, or the next person at the counter might be declaiming – it still doesn't taste good. If a wine doesn't appeal, pour it into waiting buckets and try something different. If the winery itself doesn't appeal, try another winery. Napa and Sonoma alone have more than 1000 wineries to choose from.

> **"** *I was an active wine writer, but I soon tired of searching for the ultimate adjective to properly portray the pedigree of a Pinot [Noir]. It was much more fun to drink wines than to talk about them* **"**
>
> **Don Martin, co-author of more than a dozen books on wine and travel**

Most wineries have sales rooms with wine by the bottle and by the case (12 bottles). Case discounts of 12 to 20 per cent are standard. Buying at the winery is easy and convenient, but supermarkets and discount stores very often undercut winery prices. Two exceptions: as smaller wineries have limited distribution, their wines may be available only at the winery. And many wineries have unadvertised sales on wines they need to move out but don't want to – or can't – sell through their regular retail distributors.

Most California wines are identified by winery, vintage and grape variety (Chardonnay, Cabernet Sauvignon, Merlot, Zinfandel, etc), although the European practice of blending different grapes is becoming more common.

State authorities have introduced a number of geographically defined *appellations* similar to the French *appellation controlée* system. Wines from the same *appellation* (Anderson Valley, Russian River, Carneros, Napa Valley) are likely to be similar because of similar growing conditions, but winemakers are free to create any taste that art, fermentation science and their own imaginations allow.

NORTHERN CALIFORNIA WINE COUNTRY

Treasures of the Sierra Nevada

Gold Country is where geology and geography met one of the world's most rabid group of opportunists, who called it the Mother Lode. Nestling in the well-mined Sierra Nevada foothills, quaint communities still reflect their Gold Rush architecture and style, 150 years after the event. Whether the treasure of this area was its gold or the beauty of the mountains and valleys still preserved in Yosemite National Park, no treasure map remains to provide the answer.

Treasures of the Sierra Nevada

North

↑

0		40 kms
0		20 miles

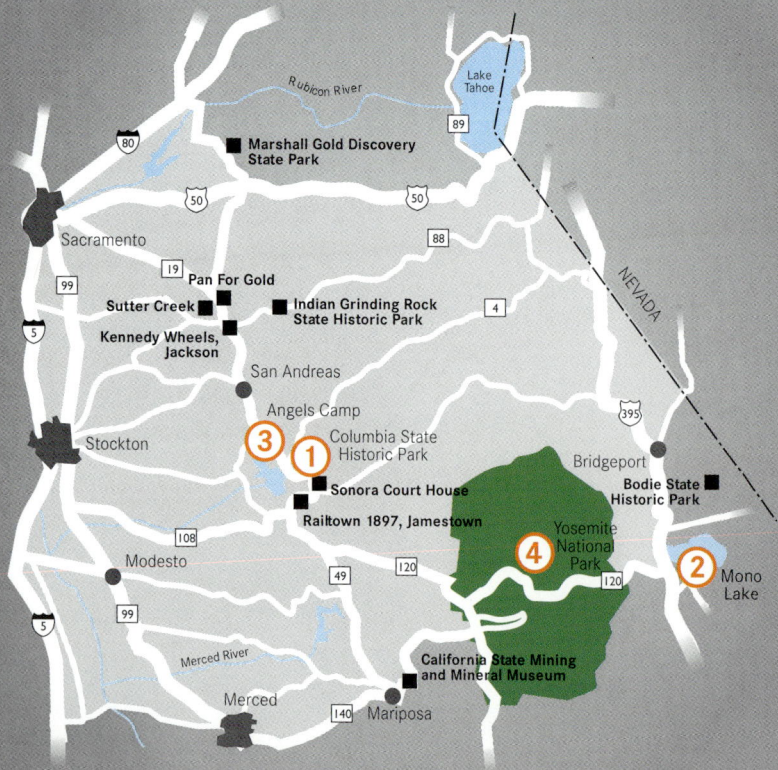

Rubicon River

Lake Tahoe

89

80

Marshall Gold Discovery State Park

50

50

88

Sacramento

99

19

Pan For Gold

Sutter Creek

Indian Grinding Rock State Historic Park

4

Kennedy Wheels, Jackson

5

San Andreas

NEVADA

Angels Camp

Stockton

③

①

Columbia State Historic Park

395

Bridgeport

Sonora Court House

Bodie State Historic Park

Railtown 1897, Jamestown

108

Yosemite National Park

④

Modesto

49

120

②

Mono Lake

120

99

5

Merced River

California State Mining and Mineral Museum

Merced

140

Mariposa

① Columbia State Historic Park

Strolling the streets of the best-preserved of all the towns in Gold Country, park rangers and volunteers evoke the era in period costume. Boardwalks front red-brick buildings along Main Street in this town that produced $87 million of 1850s gold. **Page 89**

② Mono Lake

A moonscape in lake form, Mono Lake's surreal tufa formations, crusty pillars and islands of limestone have only existed since the 1940s, a decade after Los Angeles extended the Owens Valley aqueduct north to the lake. Siphoning lake water southwards caused the water level to drop, exposing the mineral-rich limestone. **Page 91**

③ Pan for gold!

After a century and a half, there's still plenty of gold, albeit mostly not classic nugget size. Sifting a pan of Mother Lode gravel in river or stream water or resifting mounds of tailings will usually yield a tiny flake or two, a golden glitter dancing in the sun. **Page 92**

④ Yosemite National Park

Valleys, craggy peaks, waterfalls, Yosemite has it all. The American icon of the outdoors is a mecca for hikers and rock climbers. Half Dome, El Capitan, Yosemite Falls and the Ahwahnee Hotel are a magnet for millions annually, yet this can still be a park for solitude, reflection and awe. **Pages 94–95**

Getting there

Exploring Gold Country is easy: Hwy 49, named for the official Gold Rush year, 1849, begins in Oakhurst, south of Yosemite National Park, and runs 200 miles north to Grass Valley. Follow Hwy 41 northeast from Oakhurst, or Hwy 140 east from Mariposa to access the heart of the park, Yosemite Valley. Eleven miles north of Coulterville, Hwy 120 provides the northernmost Yosemite park access via Tioga Pass (*open late spring–early autumn*) to provide through access to Hwy 395 at Lee Vining (Mono Lake).

Angels Camp

Calaveras Lodging and Visitors Bureau 1211 S Main St, Angels Camp. Tel: 209-736-0049 or 800-225-3764; web: www.calaveras.org/visit.

Gold Country provided endless stories for newspaper reporters and writers who watched the world race to the dust and filth of mines. Samuel Langhorne Clemens (aka **Mark Twain**) honed his writing skills here. Never mind whether the tales were tall ones, fabrications with nuggets of truth: *The Celebrated Frog of Calaveras County*, an 1865 retelling of an age-old tale of a gullible man, is delightfully rendered in the rough, semi-educated language Twain heard. The ruby miner's finely trained frog is filled with birdshot by a rival, a fact discovered after the innocent loses a frog-jumping competition.

> *Good bye God, we're going to Bodie.*
>
> **Anonymous young girl's diary, late 19th century**

Frogtown has hosted the annual red-legged-frog **Jumping Frog Jubilee** race the third week in May at the **Calaveras County Fair** since 1928, amidst considerable hilarity and superstitious rituals to enforce amphibian performance. Frog souvenirs aside, Angels Camp was a true gold-producing centre, discovered when a miner let off his jammed muzzle-loading rifle at Main St, and found $10,000 of gold lodged in a quartz rock he'd shattered (*Calaveras County Fairgrounds, 2 miles south; tel: 209-736-2561; admission: $*).

Bodie State Historic Park

Hwy 270 (last 3 miles gravel). Tel: 760-647-6445; web: www/ceres.ca.gov/sierradsp/bodie.html. Open all year. Call for winter road closure. Self-guiding tour booklet: $.

The eastern side of the Sierra Nevada held gold in the hills, too, above a windy, tumbleweed-ridden desert. Bodie is a

ghost town of more than 100 wooden buildings falling from disrepair into total ruin (though buildings are actually chemically preserved) as the elements and time take their toll.

California State Mining and Mineral Museum

5007 Fairgrounds Rd, Mariposa. Tel: 209-742-7625; web: www.consrv.ca.gov/smmm/museum. Open Wed–Mon 1000–1800 May–Sept, Wed–Sun 1000–1600 Oct–Apr. Admission: $.

Mineral-rich California shows off some of the state's finest treasures – gold nuggets and perfect specimens of precious and semi-precious gems – in a building resembling an 1890s' mining complex. Walk through a 150ft-long gold-mine tunnel. An operational stamp mill model explains one of the common methods of rendering rock for gold extraction. Gold and California gems of the highest quality are on offer in the giftshop.

Columbia State Historic Park

Tel: 209-532-4301 or 209-532-0150; web: www.sierra.parks.state.ca.us/coconten.htm. Open daily 0900–1800.

Columbia is almost a Gold Country theme park – but not quite. Main Street is wide, lined with wooden boardwalks and red-brick, two-storey buildings. Fire destroyed most Gold Country buildings and many towns, but the result of Columbia's largest conflagration in 1854 was rebuilding in brick with iron shutters and fireproof doors. 'The Gem of the Southern Mines' yielded about $1.5 billion-worth of gold at current value, sufficient to support thousands of citizens in the 1850s.

Horses, Wells Fargo Stagecoach rides and pedestrians are permitted in the historic town peopled by rangers and workers in 1850s/1860s' costumes. Unlike a film set, the buildings are real, including the **Wells Fargo & Co Building** (a museum), the **Fallon Hotel and Theatre**, the **City Hotel**, and the **Justice Court** (a museum). The **Columbia Museum/ historic park visitor center** (*Main and State Sts; open daily 0900–1700*) has artefacts that give an excellent introduction to Columbia history and Gold Country mining methods and yields.

Kennedy Wheels and Mine

Northeast of Jackson. Tel: 209-223-9542. Mine tours: weekends Mar–Oct.
Admission: $.

From Hwy 49, 1¹/₂ miles north of Jackson, an overlook takes in the valley studded with the headframe of the Kennedy Mine. There, miners for rivals Kennedy Mining & Milling Company and the Argonaut Mine dug vertically down almost 6000ft through quartz in 100 per cent humidity and 87°F (30.5°C) in the search for gold. Fire constantly threatened one or the other mine, and shafts were close enough to affect one another's operations. A 1920 fire required co-operating crews to remove 190 million gallons of wet mud; a 1922 long-smouldering fire trapped and killed 47 men in the Argonaut.

Kennedy Mine tours include the (clothing) Change Room with mine artefacts, viewing shaft elevators, the machine ship and boiler room. Despite hardships, almost $60 million-worth of gold (value far higher today) was taken from the two mines. In 1912, **Kennedy Mine Tailing Wheels** (*N Main St, in a park 1 mile north of downtown Jackson; open daily dawn–dusk; admission: $*) were used to lift mining rubble to a dump.

Marshall Gold Discovery State Park

310 Back St, Coloma. Tel: 530-622-3470; web: www.isgnet.com/coloma. Park open daily 0800–sunset; museum open Memorial Day–Labor Day 1000–1700; call rest of year.

The epicentre of California's Gold Rush is not unusual, though the **Gold Discovery Museum/visitor centre** has fine exhibits on 'what happened here'. On the South Fork of the American River it's easy to imagine the bone-chilling cold braved by James Marshall (Sutter's Mill sawmill manager) to fetch his gold flake from the tailrace (*see page 98*). Marshall ended almost penniless and is buried on the hill above the discovery site (*off Hwy 49 to Sacramento St and Cold Springs Rd, right up Monument Rd*).

Mono Lake

This volcanic region, with its salty alkaline lake water, hosts 80 species of migratory birds which feed on the salt-adapted brine shrimp and the alkali fly. Walk the mile-long **South Tufa Trail** to see the most striking **tufa towers**. North shore tufa and marshes are visible from the **Mono Lake County Park** boardwalk.

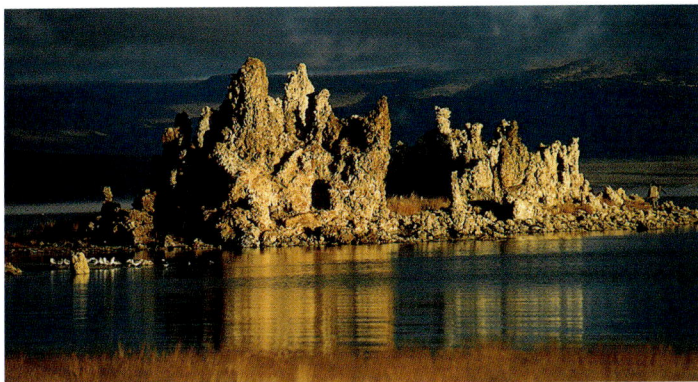

Tourist information

Mono Basin Scenic Area Visitor Center *Hwy 395, 1 mile north of Lee Vining. Tel: 760-647-3044; web: www.ceres.ca.gov/sierradsp/mono.html. Open daily 0900–1700 Apr–Oct, Thur–Mon 0900–1600 rest of year.*

Pan for gold!

Gold still comes into mountain streams from the sides of the Sierra Nevada Foothills. Anyone can pan for fun without a permit, a patient, quiet activity requiring concentration. The standard pan resembles a slope-sided metal pie tin. A small handful of grit, rocky dirt or pebbly sand, rocks removed first, is thrown in the tin with water. A deft swirling action washes the sand, grit and dirt over the side. Gold, being heaviest, will glint in the pan.

Some modern-day gold prospectors still make a living panning, or placer mining (*see pages 98–99*). **Jensen's Pick & Shovel Ranch** (*4977 Parrotts Ferry Rd, Angels Camp; tel: 209-736-0287; open daily, advance booking required; admission: $$*). and **Gold Prospecting Expeditions** (*18170 Main St, Jamestown; tel: 209-984-4653 or 800-596-0009; open daily, advance booking required; admission: $$*) offer panning opportunities.

Railtown 1897

Railtown 1897 State Historic Park two blocks east of Historic Downtown Jamestown on 5th Ave. Tel: 209-984-3953; web: www.csrmf.org/railtown. Grounds open daily 0930–1630, steam train excursions weekends Apr–Oct.

Visit film stars in this fine railway museum dedicated to the rolling stock used by the local Sierra Railway Company of California (established 1897), which hauled lumber to Jamestown, and other venerable locomotive engines, coaches and observation cars. Sierra Locomotive No 3 has starred in more than 100 films (including *Unforgiven*), changing colour(s) and stack as required. After visiting the large roundhouse and turntable, watch experts in the machine shop tooling equipment before going on to picnic or shop in the depot store, which has a fabulous collection of railway books, caps and souvenirs.

" Did I not martyrize myself into a human mule, by descending to the bottom of a dreadful pit (suffering mortal terror all the time, lest it should cave in upon me,) actuated by a virtuous desire to see with my own two eyes the process of underground mining . . . "

Louise Clapp, writing in 1852 as Dame Shirley from a log cabin at Indian Bar, *Shirley Letters from the California Mines*

Sonora

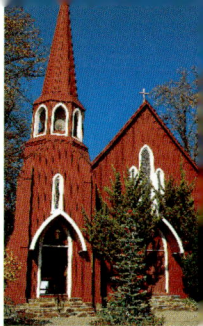

Tuolumne County Visitors Bureau 55 W Stockton Rd, Sonora. Tel: 209-533-4420 or 800-446-1333; web: www.thegreatunfenced.com. Open Apr–Oct Mon–Thur 0900–1900, Fri 0900–2000, Sat 1000–1800, Sun 1000–1700, Nov–Mar Mon–Fri 0900–1800, Sat 1000–1700.

The Queen of the Southern Mines, as Sonora was known, was a hotbed of racism against Mexicans, and one of the richest gold strike areas in the Mother Lode. The **Tuolumne County Museum** (*158 W Bradford Ave; tel: 209-532-1317; open daily 0930–1600*) is only one of many historic buildings, this one the old 1866 prison, iron bars intact, with exhibits on local Gold Rush history. One of Gold Country's icons, the 1859 rooster-red **St James Episcopal Church** (*Washington St*), stands on Piety Hill close to the Big Bonanza Mine site where, in the 1870s, a vein of solid gold yielded $660,000 of gold in a week. Sonora's oldest building, the 1850 **Gunn House** (*286 S Washington St*), which began as an adobe structure, is now an inn.

Sutter Creek

Amador County Chamber of Commerce 125-B Peek St, Jackson. Tel: 209-223-0350 or 800-649-4988; web: www.cdepot.net/chamber. Open Mon–Fri 0900–1700.

Extending a few blocks along Hwy 49, Sutter Creek's gingerbread-laced Victorian manses and two-storey wooden storefronts approached on wooden boardwalks built high against floods, lend an air of prosperity to this Gold Country town – 1851 prosperity – which somehow never burned or withered away. Bed and Breakfast Inns are amongst the best and most expensive in the region, and fill the 61 wood-

frame and brick historic buildings not used for other purposes. **Knight's Foundry** (*81 Eureka St*) fabricated much of Gold Country's heavy mining equipment.

Yosemite National Park

Box 557, Yosemite National Park. Tel: 209-372-0200; web: www.nps.gov/yose; http://www.yosemite.org. Park admission: $$.

Yosemite National Park may be as familiar as the Eiffel Tower, Big Ben or the Statue of Liberty, but the scenery remains striking.

Yosemite Valley

Yosemite and **Bridalveil Falls** rushing and pounding (or, in winter, frozen in place on the sides of sheer cliffs), **Half Dome's** shimmering white pate, **El Capitan's** vertical climbing challenge, the **Sentinel's** spike standing watch, **the wedding chapel**, the grey stone **Ahwahnee Hotel** set off by sheer cliffs behind, all are instantly recognisable from films and postcards. **Yosemite Valley**, with its loop road, is literally the park centre – filled with sights, trailheads, accommodation and camping, restaurants and a grocery store, museums and scenery galore.

The trick is to get out into nature, in the spirit of John Muir, the explorer-naturalist-godfather of Yosemite who, with his evocative writings, convinced leaders that it was worth making the former home of a few long-gone Native Americans into a national park in 1890. In 1903, US President **Teddy Roosevelt** went camping in the awesome splendour near Bridalveil Falls with Muir.

The Valley's activities are concentrated at the east end – from tubing and canoeing on the Merced River with Half Dome as a backdrop, to watching deer wandering through meadows or bears rifling (even secured) cars for comestibles, to hiking the Mist Trail to **Vernal Falls**, to a walk through wetlands to the fast-disappearing **Mirror Lake**. Except in winter, take the Badger Pass (Ski Area) road to the tunnel viewpoint near **Glacier Point**, for vistas from the *top* of the valley.

Tioga Pass

Hwy 120, **Tioga Pass Rd** (*closed mid Nov–May*), passes through the northern park areas in a 2-hour, 70-mile drive towards Lee Vining, Mono Lake (*see page 91*). The **Tuolumne** (sequoia redwood) **Grove** is accessible year-round. **Siesta Lake** reflects the mountain forests, and **Tenaya Lake** is a fisher's paradise. At 8600ft, **Tuolumne Meadows** is high country, with camping, backpacking, fishing, horse-riding and proximate rock-climbing. Hwy 120 descends quickly past alpine lakes from 9945ft **Tioga Pass**.

Southern Yosemite

Anchored by the white, Victorian-era **Wawona Hotel**, the southern end of the park offers easy access to the **Mariposa Grove of Big Trees** (*2 miles east of South Park entrance; tram: mid Apr–mid Nov 0900–1800; $*). The giant sequoias can be explored by tram or on foot. In 1899, a US Cavalry troop and steeds posed atop the **Fallen Monarch**, only one of these huge trees. Standing or fallen, they dwarf anything else living on earth.

Tourist information

Yosemite Valley Visitor Center, *Yosemite Village. Tel: 209-372-0265. Open daily 0900–1700.*
Tuolumne Meadows Visitor Center, *Tuolumne Meadows. Tel: 209-372-0263. Open daily early summer–Sept.*

Eating out in Gold Country

Gold Country economy depends upon its Bed and Breakfasts, hotels, motels, restaurants and country stores selling souvenirs, jams, candles and replica Victorian bric-à-brac. Some Gold Country towns, such as Sutter Creek, close restaurants and shops for part of the week, even during summer high season.

Yosemite National Park welcomes approximately 5 million visitors annually, most arriving in Yosemite Valley between June and mid-September. Snow arrives early, especially in the mountain passes, but autumn to early spring can be lovely, almost deserted, a wonderland shared only with those who appreciate more subtle seasons.

Here are a few of the best 'rest and refresh' spots in Gold Country and Yosemite National Park.

Columbia State Historic Park

Fallon Hotel and City Hotel

Tel: 209-532-1479 or 800-532-1479; web: www.cityhotel.com, both on Main St. $$$. These two historic hotels operate as cosy Bed and Breakfasts, though without en-suite bath.

The City Hotel Dining Room

City Hotel, Main St. Tel: 209-532-1479 or 800-532-1479. $$$. The best cuisine in Gold Country has an appreciative clientele which reserves in advance for French with *nouvelle* California ingredients.

What Cheer Saloon

Main St, adjacent to the City Hotel. Libations have been served here since the 1870s when the City Hotel went by this name.

Douglas Saloon

Main St. Try a sarsaparilla; even if you're no longer a child, the sweetened, carbonated brewed bark drink is refreshing on warm summer days.

Sonora

Ryan House

153 S Shepherd St. Tel: 209-533-3445 or 800-831-4897; web: www.ryanhouse.com. $$. Built by Irish immigrants who escaped the mid-19th-century potato famine, this Bed and Breakfast inn is renowned for its breakfast scones and cheer.

Good Heavens: A Food Concern

49 N Washington St. Tel: 209-532-3663. Lunch Tue–Sun. $$. Once there were coffins downstairs, ladies of the evening upstairs. This lunch spot serves food these days, freshly made baked goods garnished with home-made jams, soups, sandwiches and crêpes.

Sutter Creek

The Foxes in Sutter Creek

77 Main St. Tel: 209-267-5882 or 800-987-3344; web: www.foxesinn.com. $$$. Lovely flower gardens front the seven-room Bed and Breakfast inn furnished with Victorian antiques. Breakfast is served in the room or garden gazebo.

Grey Gables Inn

161 Hanford St. Tel: 209-267-1039 or 800-473-9422; web: www.cdepot.net/ greygables. $$. British writers' and poets' names grace the eight rooms of this Bed and Breakfast run by British expatriates.

Zinfandels

51 Hanford St. Tel: 209-267-5008. $$$. Local wines complement delicately prepared California cuisine's fresh ingredients at this restaurant.

Yosemite

All park accommodation booking is arranged by **Yosemite Reservations** (*5410 East Home, Fresno; tel: 209-252-4848*).

The Ahwahnee Hotel

($$$). The multi-storey 'rustic' resort hotel built of cliff-matching grey granite in 1927 is posh in décor, especially the large and colourful Native American and Afghan rugs which decorate the fireplace-warmed Great Hall. The vast Dining Room resembles a cathedral nave, with wooden vaulting supporting large view windows and huge chandeliers.

"*You've heard the stories about YOSEMITE. Too many people, right? Bears raid your food every night, right? Your vacation turns into an endurance test called You Against the World. That's what kept me away for 20 years . . . it took only five minutes in YOSEMITE VALLEY to turn our attitudes around 180 degrees, leaving us completely under the spell of the world's greatest natural showpiece.*"

Tom Stienstra, *Outdoor Getaway Guide: Northern California*

Going for the gold

The Gold Rush of 1848–9 yielded the largest supply of gold the world had seen since Spain looted the Aztec and Inca empires of South America two centuries earlier. California's gold seekers didn't dig and run. The Argonauts, as they were called, came, dug for gold and stayed.

The original discovery was fantasy come to life. In January 1848, James Marshall saw bits of a shiny, golden substance glinting in the freezing waters of the American River while building a water-powered sawmill. As word of Marshall's discovery spread, nearly every able-bodied person in California raced for the foothills of the Sierra Nevada. Before transcontinental railways or even telegraph lines, it took months for news of gold to reach the eastern US, Europe, South America and Asia. It was quicker for prospectors to sail as far as Panama, cross the isthmus on foot and sail north, but malaria, yellow fever and dysentery killed thousands along the way.

The dream of gold transcended every hardship. California's climate was benign, but mining, successful or not, was back-breaking labour. Once surface nuggets had been picked clean, gold seekers began **placer mining**, sifting through streambeds for color, as small flecks of gold were called.

" Governor Richard B Mason should have declared California a disaster area on January 24, 1848. For Jim Marshall's discovery of gold that day on the South Fork of the American River blew open a bottomless Pandora's box whose lid has never since been found, much less closed. "

Richard Dillon, introduction to *Humbugs and Heroes, A Gallery of California Pioneers*

Individual miners could **pan** for gold, using a swirling motion to **wash** river dirt and gravel in pans that looked like oversized pie tins. Water washed away the lighter gravel, dirt and sand, leaving behind the heavier gold. Groups of miners banded together to build **long toms**, **cradles** and **sluice boxes**, devices that washed gold-bearing gravel over boxes with cross-pieces fixed to the bottom to catch the heavier pieces of gold. Miners diverted streams and rivers to gain access to what they hoped was **pay dirt**, sometimes sinking shafts to reach ancient streambeds covered by aeons of erosion. Enormous **dredges** became a common sight along rivers and larger streams, leaving behind heaps of rubble – tailings – that still scar the landscape.

Hard rock mines used traditional mining techniques to follow veins of gold deep beneath the Sierra Nevada. Gold-bearing ore was pounded into dust in **stamp mills** and the metal was extracted using mercury amongst other poisonous chemicals. **Hydraulic mines** left entire mountainsides blasted into badlands by the force of rivers channelled through gigantic nozzles called **monitors**. The run-off was directed through enormous sluice boxes which extracted the largest chunks of gold. The residue was left to run into streams, rivers and, eventually, into San Francisco Bay.

The Great Western Desert

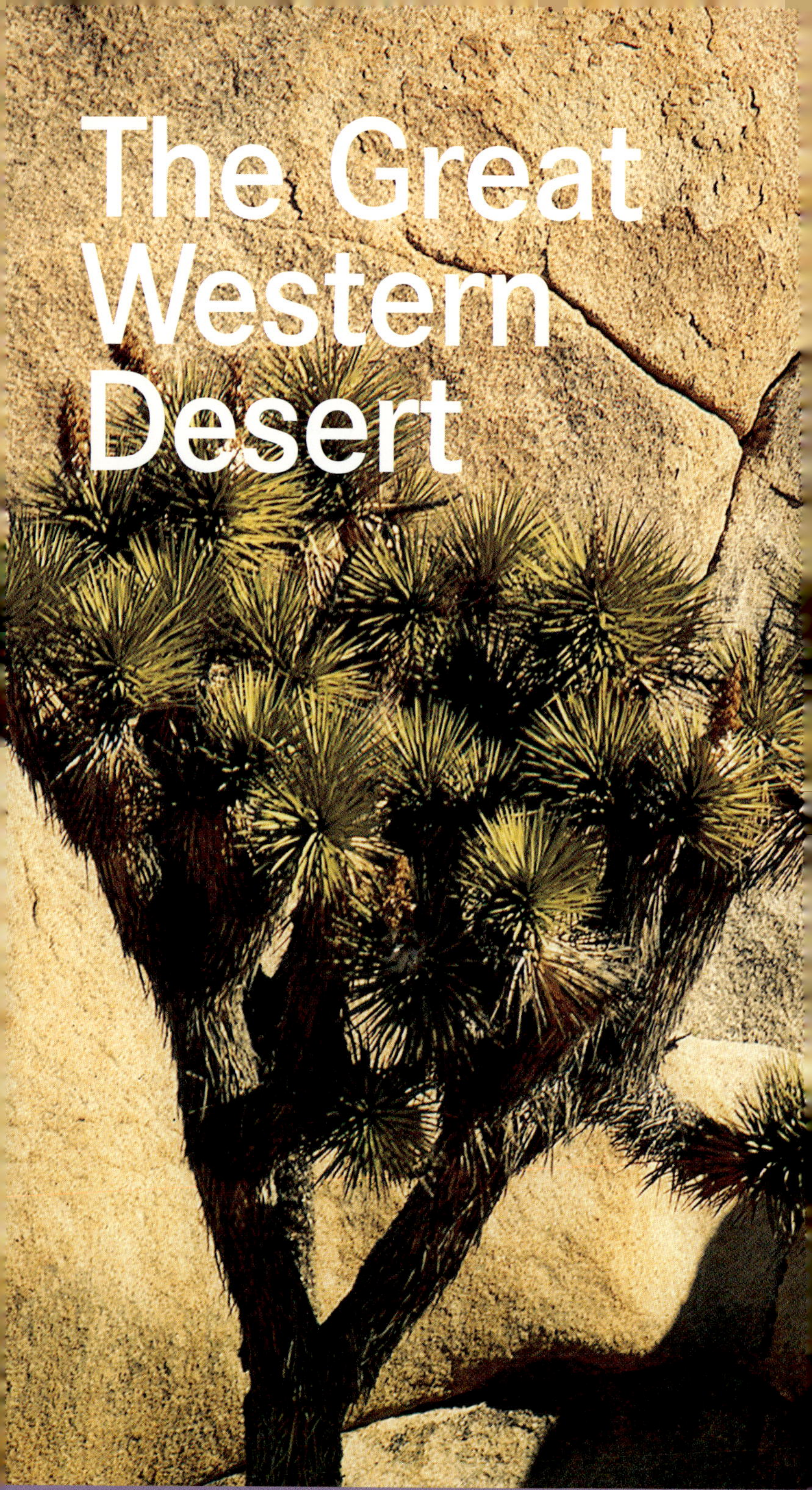

Nowhere is a moonrise more spectacular than over a desert spiked by mountain ranges that pierce the disk as it rises. Cacti and heaven-pointing Joshua trees create multi-armed, almost human silhouettes. Many-coloured sands shift into dunes, sifted into patterns by a faint, constant, silent wind. A hell on earth to early settlers trying to cross it, the vast desert of California is the least-explored area of the state.

THE GREAT WESTERN DESERT

BEST OF
The Great Western Desert

North
↑

Death Valley National Park:
Artists Drive, Badwater,
Dante's View, Sand Dunes,
Scotty's Castle, Ubehebe

190

395

Zabriskie
Point ③

178

Death Valley
National
Park

127

NEVADA

LAKE
MEAD

14

Mojave National Preserve
Cima Dome & Joshua Trees

58

Barstow

15

Kelso Dunes

MOJAVE
NATIONAL
RESERVE

④

395

15

40

Mitchell Caverns
Provincial Mountains
State Recreation Area

Needles

San Bernardino

Riverside

Cholla Cactus Garden
Jumbo Rocks

10

95

Colorado River

Santa Ana

Palm Springs Aerial Tramway
Indian Canyons, Palm Springs

⑤ ②

Joshua Tree
National Park

Palm Desert, El Paseo (shopping)
Living Desert

⑥ ①

79

Date
Milkshake

10

Oceanside

15

Font's Point

Salton Sea

Blythe

PACIFIC
OCEAN

San Diego

Anza-Borrego
Desert
State Park

ARIZONA

Tijuana

MEXICO

Yuma

0 — 100 kms
0 — 50 miles

① Font's Point, Anza-Borrego Desert State Park

Coloured sandstone canyon badlands spread below a viewpoint with views to the Salton Sea in California's largest state park. **Page 105**

② Date milkshake

East of Palm Springs and Palm Desert, in Indio, are groves of date palms. The creamy, delicious recipe for milkshakes using sweet local dates hasn't changed in 50 years. **Page 105**

③ Zabriskie Point, Death Valley National Park

Manly Beacon, a point of land pushed sideways aeons ago, marks the famous spot which catches first light when the sun rises pinkly over the mountains east of the valley. **Page 107**

④ Kelso Dunes, Mojave National Preserve

The huge dunes boom, or sing, with the shifting goldenrod-coloured sands. Hike to the ridgetop to slide down the edge of a dune. **Page 109**

⑤ Golf in Palm Springs

World-famous golfers plan the courses where film stars and entertainers play tournaments for pleasure and charity. Rough mountains are a backdrop to palm-tree-lined courses, as the Coachella Valley cities yield the right of way to golf carts. **Page 110**

⑥ Indian canyons

Native Americans preserve their traditional canyonlands south of the city of Palm Springs. Shady streamside palms provide a green oasis for walkers and horse-riders in one canyon. **Page 111**

Getting there

California's southeast corner is desert. For Anza-Borrego Desert State Park, take I-8 east of San Diego, turn north on Hwy 79 for 24 miles, then go east on Hwy 78, following signs to park areas. Palm Springs, Palm Desert and Indio are southeast of Los Angeles via I-10, which also provides south-side access to Joshua Tree National Park further east. I-40 and I-15 provide respective south and north access to Mojave National Preserve. Take Hwy 178 or 190 east from Hwy 395 to enter Death Valley National Park from the west.

103

Anza-Borrego Desert State Park

Spectacular in a year of prime wildflower bloom (Wildflower Hotline Jan–Mar season tel: 760-767-4684), this largest state park in the 48 United States has 600,000 acres of wilderness surrounding Borrego Springs, a town with visitor services.

The visitor centre is built, cave-like, into the rock, well insulated from the blistering summer heat. A well-adapted pupfish population survives in a nearby pond (and another pond near the Borrego Palm Canyon trailhead). Volunteers maintain a desert botanical garden of cacti and trees characteristic of this Colorado Desert section of the Sonoran Desert. Check with rangers for roads requiring four-wheel drive, and restrictions on mountain biking or closures on the 500 miles of park roads.

Borrego Palm Canyon hike

Loop north of the visitor centre to park just beyond the Borrego Palm Canyon camp ground.

Trail highpoints are described in a self-guiding brochure from the trailhead box. Plan on 3 hours to hike the 3-mile

return trail. The shaded oasis at the end of the trail is ideal for a picnic near a pool fed by a waterfall. Trees at the trail terminus are native California fan palms, thick and bushy with fronds; the mantle of withered leaves makes a rustling sheath around the trunk. Along the trail are colourful rocks, red-flowering, thorny-stemmed ocotillo, barrel cacti, golden boulders, a rushing stream, and perhaps the rare peninsular bighorn sheep, the borrego, which lend the park half its name.

Font's Point

In a sturdy car with high clearance, drive east past the Borrego Springs Airport, north on Peg Leg Rd, and east onto Hwy 22, the Erosion Road Trail. At mile marker 23, turn south 4 miles over and through very rough dirt and sand, framed by eroded alluvial fans.

Sunset and sunrise turn the brownish Borrego Badlands crevasses south and east of the edge of the cliff a shimmering rose pink. Sunset is almost a spectator sport, with a small crowd of amiable couples in beach or lawn chairs, tables laden with drinks and snacks at the ready. The bluish-white Salton Sea sparkles to the east on clearer afternoons. A favourite photo spot, Font's Point photos make human subjects appear atop a surreal inversion layer of colour. Inevitably, sun-watchers are drawn to the canyon's unprotected edge – do not back up!

Shields Date Gardens

80225 Hwy 111, Indio. Tel: 760-347-0996 or 800-414-2555. Open daily 0800–1800 Sept–May, 0900–1700 June–Aug.

In the 1920s, several couples set up date stands with gardens to sell the dates produced from groves 'out back'. Young plants were imported from Algeria and elsewhere in North Africa. **Shields Date Gardens** continues to sell local citrus and 119 different date varieties, by catalogue and from a shop whose décor is frozen in the 1940s. After seeing the slightly amusing 1950s film, *The Romance and Sex Life of the Date*, step up to the ice-cream fountain and order a date shake (*$*): cool, refreshing and creamy, laced with sweet date bits.

Anza-Borrego Desert State Park, 200 Palm Canyon Dr, Borrego Springs. Tel: 760-767-4205 or 760-767-5311. Visitors Center 5 miles west of Christmas Circle, Borrego Springs. Open daily 0900–1700 Oct–May, weekends and holidays June–Sept. Admission: $, visitor centre free.

Death Valley National Park

Box 579, Death Valley. Tel: 760-786-2331; web: www.nps.gov/deva. Park admission: $$.

Pioneers wandered the harsh Death Valley desert in the 19th century; miners sought gold and produced borax carried away by 20-mule team caravans. Modern bicyclists brave hideous summer heat. Scenery, flowers, mountains, sand and colour – Death Valley has it all in huge proportions.

Artists Drive

9 miles south of Furnace Creek, left off Badwater Rd.

The route rises above the shimmering white, flat valley floor to skirt mountainsides painted with pink, green, yellow and red, coloured by minerals. The Artists Palette turnoff is to the right about halfway along Artists Drive, an intense, panoramic display of rock colours in one spot.

Badwater

16$^{1}/_{2}$ miles south of Furnace Creek.

Pull into the parking area for a view of the lowest place in the Western Hemisphere, 279.8ft below sea level. A simple park sign marks 'Badwater' and the elevation; it's instinctive to go close to the sign, take a photo, and then to walk west on the blindingly white alkali path into the middle of lowness, in the heart of Death Valley's floor.

Dante's View

Hwy 190 12$^{1}/_{2}$ miles south of Furnace Creek; turn right at Dante's View Road.

Borax was mined here, but the attraction is the view from 5475ft above sea level, 13 miles south and east of the turnoff. The *Inferno*-style view extends west from Badwater in the valley below to the Panamint Mountains with 11,049ft Telescope Peak and a hint of the Sierra Nevada range beyond.

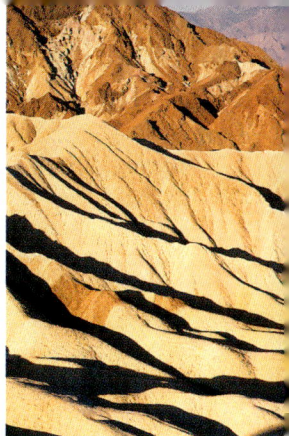

Sand dunes

Two areas of sheer sand dunes rise in Death Valley National Park. The Eureka Dunes are remote, 98 miles north of Furnace Creek via Hwy 90 and rugged dirt roads. The much more easily accessible sand dunes near Stovepipe Wells are visible for miles. Either area is most dramatic at dawn or just before sunset, when shadows are long and the classic curving ridge lines are defined by shadowed blackness.

Scotty's Castle

53 miles north of Furnace Creek via Hwy 190. Tel: 760-786-2392. Open daily 0830–1700. Tour: $.

Sold on Death Valley's gold-mining possibilities, flamboyant and affable self-promoter Walter Scott used funds from a business tycoon friend to construct a home in the desert between 1922 and 1931. Costumed rangers conduct hourly living-history tours of the whitewashed Moorish-style home.

Ubehebe Crater

West of Scotty's Castle; 5 miles west of the Grapevine Park Entrance.

The volcanic orange depression, 600ft deep and 2600ft wide, with a 30° slope, exploded into shape about 3000 years ago. A trail circles the rim.

Zabriskie Point

4 miles SE of Furnace Creek on Hwy 190.

Gold and pink-coloured mountains pick up the first rays of the sun as it rises and highlights Manly Beacon. Pre-dawn temperatures can be freezing for watchers who park and walk a few hundred feet up to the Zabriskie Point overlook. Once dawn arrives, the colour washes out quickly.

Tourist information

Furnace Creek Visitor Center and Museum (*tel: 760-786-2331; open daily 0800–1800*). **Visitor Centers** at **Stovepipe Wells** and **Scotty's Castle** (*open daily 0800–1700*).

Joshua Tree National Park

74485 National Park Dr, Twentynine Palms. Tel: 760-367-5500; web: www.nps.gov/jotr. Admission: $.

The cooler, damper Mojave Desert meets another hotter, drier, lower desert – the Colorado – at White Tank. The transition zone between the Mojave's golden boulders set off by Joshua trees and the sparer cholla (pronounced *choy-uh*) vegetation is dramatic.

Cholla Cactus Garden

Pinto Basin Rd

The 'teddy bear' cholla (*Opuntia bigelovii*) may look innocuous, fenced behind low wooden corral posts on the self-guiding trail. These are 'jumping' cholla, the pin-sharp spiny needles seeming to leap into the skin – even breaching rubber-soled shoes. Yellow-green flowers bunch at the ends of cacti branches. Mixed with creosote bush, the cholla shelter big-eared black-tailed jackrabbits below and cactus wrens in its branches and skeletons. At dusk, the cholla look like a pygmy army marching into the pink Pinto Basin.

Jumbo Rocks

Follow Park Blvd as it veers west.

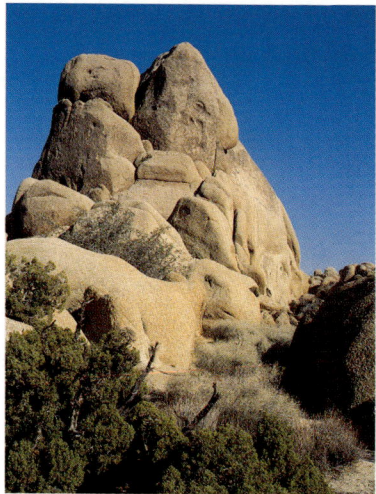

Golden granite? Huge jumbles of jumbo? Agglomerations of fissured rock rise in clumps around the **Jumbo Rocks Campground**. Jumbo rock outcroppings are dramatic at nearby **Split Rock** and at the eerie **Skull Rock**, obvious on the boulevard's south side. Rock climbers head west of Jumbo Rocks to **Ryan Campground**, **Hidden Valley** or the balancing **Cap Rock**, surrounded by Joshua tree forest.

Kelso Dunes

South of Kelso, 3 miles west off Kelbaker Rd.

Enter a surreal countryside of 600ft-high wind-formed sand ridges, shimmering yellow or white in the changing light. More than 40 square miles of dunes shift constantly, the momentum building up to an imitation of a faint sonic boom, the song of the dunes. Early morning is best for spotting animal and snake tracks; watch the reflected setting sun glow pink on the Providence Mountains to the east.

Mitchell Caverns

Northeast of I-40 7 miles on Essex Rd, turn west for 5 miles. Providence Mountains State Recreation Area, Box 1, Essex. Tel: 760-928-2586. Caverns and park admission: $$.

The view from the park visitor centre, 4300ft above the eastern preserve, extends 100 miles into Nevada. Guided 1½-hour cavern tours, comfortable at a year-round 65°F (18°C), highlight stalactites and stalagmites which have stopped growing, limited by the dry desert climate outside.

Joshua tree

The spiky national park namesake, Yucca brevifolia, *is a lily, not a cactus. Queen Valley has the oldest tree, 40ft tall and 900 years old.*

Palm Desert

Palm Springs Desert Resorts Convention and Visitors Bureau
69-930 Hwy 111, Ste 201, Rancho Mirage. Tel: 760-770-9000;
web: www.desert-resorts.com. Visitor Center open daily 0830–1730.

El Paseo

One block south, parallels Hwy 111. From Hwy 74 to Portola Ave.

A 2-mile-long shopping street offers Beverly Hills' Rodeo Drive or Florida's Palm Beach posh boutiques and galleries without the fuss. Retired socialites patronise more than 150 shops alongside urban professionals and tourists. Look to outdoor malls such as **Gardens on El Paseo** (*tel: 760-862-1990*), for alfresco concerts. Drop into the **Museum at the Gardens** (*tel: 760-325-0189*) an annex of the **Palm Springs Desert Museum**. **CODA Gallery** offerings are as fine as any museum's (*73-151 El Paseo; tel: 760-346-4661 or 800-700-4661*).

Living Desert Wildlife & Botanical Park

47-900 Portola Ave, Palm Desert. Tel: 760-346-5694; web: www.livingdesert.org.
Open daily 0900–1630 Sept–mid-June, varies mid-June–Aug. Admission: $$.

Experience California desert vegetation and desert fauna from around the world in a 1200-acre almost-zoo laced with pathways that lead from one kind of cacti to another. Endangered golden eagles, mountain lions and bobcats live in Eagle Canyon. The WaTuTu village replicates a Kenyan village, with domestic cattle and savannah species, such as amur leopards and striped hyenas.

Golf

Dry weather, sunshine, desert mountain scenery and lots of space create one of the world's great golfing meccas, with almost 100 courses. Palm Desert is the first US city to develop a golf-cart transportation system, which allows access to courses and city streets, and trots out golf-cart 'floats' for the annual November Golf Parade. The world watches the **Bob Hope Chrysler Classic** *(3rd week Jan). Golf shops are rife; for golf history and artefacts visit the* **Jude E Poynter Golf Museum** *(* Institute of Golf Management, Fred Waring Dr between Monterey and San Pablo Aves; tel 760-341-2491 *).*

Palm Springs

Palm Springs lends its name and image to the valley. Native Americans own a chequerboard of land and a spa-casino in town in one of the greatest land coups in American history.

Aerial Tramway

One Tramway Rd. Tel: 760-325-1391 or 888-515-8726; web: www.pstramway.com. Open Mon–Fri 1000–2145, Sat–Sun 0800–2145. Admission: $$$.

Get 8516ft above the Southern California desert, 6000ft above the valley floor, in rotating 360°-view gondola cars. Admire the view from the top, visit the cafeteria, and hike, ride a mule or, in winter, Nordic ski in the 13,000-acre Mount San Jacinto State Park behind the tramway complex.

Indian canyons

End of south Palm Canyon Dr. Tel: 760-325-1053 or 800-790-3398; web: www.aguacaliente.org. Open 0800–1700 Sept–Mar, 0800–1800 Apr–Aug. Admission: $.

The Aqua Caliente Band of Cahuilla Indians protect their four canyons south of the city of Palm Springs as a sacred trust. **Palm Canyon**, lined with California fan palm is a prime area for picnicking, horse-riding (**Smoke Tree Stables**, *tel: 760-327-1372; $$*), and hiking. A Trading

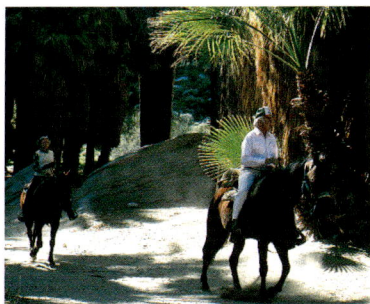

Post offers Native American baskets, jewellery and crafts. **Andreas Canyon**, with hiking trails, has more palms than any other in the world except Palm Canyon. Hike through **Murray Canyon** to spot bighorn sheep, wild ponies and California tree frogs. At **Tahquitz Canyon** the visitor centre will offer views and tribal artefacts excavated near by in a previously private area.

Tourist information

Palm Springs Tourism *333 N Palm Canyon Dr, Ste 114, Palm Springs. Tel: 760-778-8415 or 800-347-7746; web: www.palm-springs.org.*
Visitor Center *2781 N Palm Canyon Dr (at Hwy 111). Open daily 0900–1730.*

Eating out in the desert

Desert heat and long, parching summers dictate the desert lifestyle. Spas in Palm Springs make sense, where climate alone seems to leach out the poisons. Desert populations concentrate in a few cities and towns, notably the Coachella Valley corridor from Palm Springs to Indio. Except for that valley, don't expect nightlife outside of bars where imbibing is the entertainment.

Anza-Borrego Desert State Park

This huge park is blessed by a town/population base at its centre. **Borrego Springs Chamber of Commerce** (*622 Palm Canyon Dr, Borrego Springs; tel: 800-559-5524; web: www.borregosprings.com; open daily 1000–1600*). Camp in the park at **Borrego Palm Canyon and Tamarisk Grove** (*tel: 800-444-7275*).

The Coffee & Book Store

590 Palm Canyon Dr. Tel: 760-767-5080. Open 0600–1800. $$. Muffins, baked goods, excellent coffee and an eclectic array of books ranging from best-sellers to desert geology are served.

Krazy Coyote Saloon & Grille

2220 Hoberg Rd. Tel: 760-767-7788 or 800-519-2624. $$$. Desert views and house-made sangria win a following for this breakfast–dinner spot.

La Casa del Zorro Desert Resort Hotel

3845 Yaqui Pass Rd. Tel: 760-767-5323 or 800-824-1884. $$$. Posh *casitas*, tennis, a spa, candlelit dining and jazz weekends (*May–Dec*) prevail at this just-out-of-town resort.

Palm Canyon Resort

221 Palm Canyon Dr. Tel: 760-767-5341 or 800-242-0044. $$. At the park doorstep, this Western-themed hotel/RV park/restaurant provides an excellent base.

Death Valley National Park

Dining in Death Valley is limited; if planning to picnic, stock up with provisions that will stay fresh and won't dry out before entering the park. The Ranch and Stovepipe Wells have grocery stores with limited stock. For **park camping** *tel: 800-365-2267 from 0700 to 1900 PST.*

Furnace Creek Inn

Furnace Creek. Tel: 760-786-2361; web: www.furnacecreekresort.com. $$$. Death Valley's most expensive lodging has lovely rooms, desert views, an outdoor pool and a fine dining restaurant.

Furnace Creek Ranch

Furnace Creek. Tel: 760-786-2345; web: www.furnacecreekresort.com. $$. The park activity centre includes motel-style lodging, a golf course, tennis courts, stables, swimming pools, post office, giftshop/grocery store, laundromat, casual restaurants and bars, petrol station and the Borax Museum.

Panamint Springs (*Hwy 190, Panamint Springs; tel: 702-482-7680; $$*) and **Stovepipe Wells Village** (*Stovepipe Wells; tel: 760-786-2387; $$*) both offer a motel, RV park, casual restaurant and a petrol station.

Joshua Tree National Park

First-come, first-served park camping is on offer. Stay in Twentynine Palms, **Twentynine Palms Chamber of Commerce** (*6455 Mesquite Ave; tel: 760-367-3445*) or south in Palm Springs/Coachella Valley.

Don's American B.B.Q.

72183 29 Palms Hwy. Tel: 760-367-0301. $$. Everything from huge steaks to seafood to chicken to all-American ribs is mesquite wood grilled outside – you can't miss the enticing odours.

The 29 Palms Inn

23950 Inn Ave. Tel: 760-367-3505. $$–$$$. Secluded, closest to the park, and renowned for its steaks, seafood and chicken.

Mojave National Preserve

The preserve has first-come, first-served camping; for **Providence Mountains SRA camping** *tel: 619-928-2586.* **Baker** (*I-15*) has several motels and restaurants, including **Bun Boy Motel** (*tel: 760-733-4363; $*) and **Bun Boy Restaurant** (*tel: 760-733-4660; $*).

Palm Springs

Palm Springs Desert Resorts CVB offer a free booking service. *Tel: 800-417-3529, for Coachella Valley accommodation and golf.*

La Quinta Resort & Club

49499 Eisenhower Dr, La Quinta. Tel: 760-564-4111 or 800-598-3828; web: www.LaQuintaResort.com. $$$. Flowers spill over Spanish-style buildings; the famed golf course has one of the most spectacular mountain backdrops anywhere.

Spa Hotel & Casino

100 N Indian Canyon Dr, Palm Springs. Tel: 760-325-1461 or 800-854-1279; web: www.aguacaliente.org/spa.html. $$$. The Aqua Caliente Band of Cahuilla Indians has taken a traditional medicinal springs site for gaming, dining and accommodation in the centre of Palm Springs.

113

"The sun reigns, I am drowned in light . . . In this glare of brilliant emptiness, in this arid intensity of pure heat, in the heart of a weird solitude, great silence and grand desolation, all things recede to distances out of reach, reflecting light but impossible to touch, annihilating all thought and all that men have made to a spasm of whirling dust far out on the golden desert."

Edward Abbey, *Desert Solitaire*

Sand surfin' safari

California's blonde surfers have never seen waves as tall as the curving ridges of shimmering desert sand dunes in Mojave National Preserve and Death Valley. Rock-climbers are challenged by Joshua Tree National Park's jagged jumbo rocks' isolation, no spectators around to cheer as when they scale Yosemite National Park's El Capitan. No botanical garden can match the blooms of barrel cacti, ocotillo, yucca and daisies in a wet winter along the canyon slopes in Anza-Borrego Desert State Park. There are fewer people visiting deserts, too, creating a place to decompress.

Some decompress halfway with a sojourn in Palm Springs, super-indulging with balmy-weather golf, spirited tennis, spa treatments, alfresco pavement dining and shopping in designer boutiques. Palm trees, warm, dry breezes, green golf courses, manicured lawns, colourful flower plantings, all create an oasis with deserts to the south and north.

Death Valley bears a name to reckon with: in 1849 settlers straggled across the US hoping to find an easier southern route to California's gold fields, an event annually commemorated by thousands of campers in the **Death Valley '49ers Encampment** in mid-November. The pioneers braved other mountains and deserts, but nothing as sere as this long, seemingly savage and empty valley.

A few prospectors looked for gold and precious minerals in the deserts; perhaps a few found

wealth in the coloured landscape which screamed of chemical riches. Borax, used as a washing compound, a flux by goldsmiths, a glaze for porcelain fabricators, and by glaziers, was the California deserts' white gold. Harmony Borax Works ruins and a wooden hauling cart from the 20-mule wagon train remain in Death Valley as haunting reminders of the harsh desert prospector-entrepreneurs faced.

So, why take a Holiday in Hell with summer heat well over 120°F (49°C) and nights below freezing? Cars with air-conditioning ease the exposure; water, liquids and planning exertion for early in the day help. Hike early to see small rodents, the threatened California (state reptile) Desert Tortoise, snakes, cactus wrens, big-eared jackrabbits, foxes, fringe-toed lizards, all scurrying across the dunes for protection under cacti or clumps of fragrant sage or above to vantage points in the seared skeletons of cholla cactus or Joshua trees.

> **"** *Folds upon folds of dunes spread beyond their shelter. Away from the setting sun, the dunes exposed greased shadows so black they were like bits of night.*
> *And the flatness.*
> *His mind searched for something tall in that landscape. But there was no persuading tallness out of heat-addled air and that horizon – no bloom or gently shaken thing to mark the passage of a breeze . . . only dunes and that distant cliff beneath a sky of burnished silver-blue.* **"**

Frank Herbert (who spent ten years as a *San Francisco Examiner* reporter), *Dune*

The seemingly inhospitable, blasted landscape of rocky hardscrabble is shockingly deceptive. The desert is actually teeming with creatures such as the desert pupfish, swimming in 111°F (44°C) waters five times saltier than the seas. Stand at Badwater surrounded by the chalky whiteness of the salt pan and *feel* the lowest place in the western hemisphere. Northwest, over the Panamint Mountains, rises the Sierra Nevada's 14,494ft Mount Whitney, the *highest* point in the hemisphere south of Alaska.

115

California's Golden Coast

The Central California Coast from Santa Cruz south to Santa Barbara is golden – the way light plays on the sand and cliffs – punctuated by aquamarine water, mysterious fogs and serpentine roads. Sophisticated resorts and wealthy enclaves hide amidst cypresses and pines, just over the ridge perhaps from meditation-begotten spas, a mogul's castle or a secluded beach.

BEST OF

California's Golden Coast

North

↑

| 0 | | 100 kms |
| 0 | | 50 miles |

Santa Cruz

Monterey Bay
Aquarium

③ Salinas

④ ③

17-Mile Drive

⑤ Monterey

Carmel

① LOS PADRES NATIONAL FOREST

King City

Big Sur Coast

Fresno

152

5

99

198

Visalia

Hearst Castle

②

PACIFIC
OCEAN

46

Paso Robles

101

5

99

46

101

San Luis Obispo

Nipomo Dunes
Preserve

Santa Maria

5

La Purisima Mission
Lompoc

1

Solvang

LOS PADRES
NATIONAL FOREST

101

Santa Barbara

① Big Sur Coast

Beaches, golden cliffs and forests alternate along California's most scenic stretch of coastline. The highway is narrow, the speed limit slow, the curves treacherous, and the lay-bys many – each one begs to be used. The 90-mile drive can easily take most of a day. **Pages 120–121**

② Hearst Castle

A California newspaper baron built a castle-size retreat with exotic animals in pasture below as a getaway for his movie-star mistress and himself. Tour individual floors and the gardens of this opulent, spare-no-expense mansion, with views from the rolling hills down to the ocean. **Page 122**

③ Monterey Bay

Beyond the shops and restaurants of Monterey's Fisherman's Wharf or Cannery Row, get up close to birds, seals and lively sea otters who demonstrate how to eat abalone from one of the richest marine sealife areas in the world. **Page 123**

④ Monterey Bay Aquarium

With a nod to the sardine cannery history of Monterey's Cannery Row, this trend-setting aquarium showed the world how to handle and display sealife from its own waters, from the long-stemmed kelp beds to rich-coloured tidepools at the shoreline. **Page 123**

⑤ 17-Mile Drive

World-famous golf courses are the icing on the cake of this not-quite-17-mile-long drive along the Pebble Beach coastline, one of California's few toll roads. The coastline just west has cliffs, sand dunes and rocks where gulls, cormorants and seals congregate, and the Pebble Beach Company signature Lone Cypress Tree. **Page 127**

Getting there

Hwy 1 hugs the coast south from San Francisco to Santa Cruz, dips inland towards Soquel and returns to the coast at Monterey. Follow Hwy 1 south (with a recommended detour south of Pacific Grove along the 17-Mile Drive to Carmel) along the Big Sur Coast to San Luis Obispo. Take Hwy 101 7 miles south. Rejoin Hwy 1 at Pismo Beach; at the Vandenburg Air Force Base turn-off, take Hwy 246 towards La Purisima Mission and on to Solvang. Return 5 miles west on Hwy 246 to Hwy 101 and continue south to Santa Barbara. From Los Angeles, go north on Hwy 101 to Santa Barbara.

Big Sur Coast

Big Sur is loosely defined as the 90 miles from south of Point Lobos State Reserve (Carmel) to San Simeon State Park and Hearst Castle. The 'Big South' is a long coastline of undeveloped and rural areas with cow pastures and soft, rolling hills, dotted with occasional million-dollar mansions hanging precariously onto cliffs.

California's coastline is public, lending Big Sur's relatively deserted beaches the cachet of being almost hidden, a true getaway from San Francisco, about 150 miles north, and from Los Angeles, about 200 miles south of San Simeon. Inland, the 167,000-acre Ventana Wilderness scales the rugged Santa Lucia Mountains, with steep V-shaped valleys, waterfalls and challenging hiking.

Coastal fog is likely to blanket the area off the Pacific Ocean for hours or days at a time – even in summer. Though cool, the fog lends an air of mystery and lovely isolation to the coast and drive, while obscuring details of nearby beaches and cliffs. Stop on the frequent lay-bys to spot or hear the barking of colonies of seals and sea lions on the beaches and shallow rocks offshore.

Andrew Molera State Park

20 miles south of Carmel.
Web: http://www.cal-parks.ca.gov/DISTRICTS/monterey/amsp.htm.

Hike, beachcomb, ride a horse, or camp near the Big Sur River, which runs through the park.

Garrapata State Park

10 miles south of Carmel. Tel: 831-624-4909;
web: http://www.cal-parks.ca.gov/DISTRICTS/monterey/gsp.htm.

Flat beaches, Soberanes Point headlands and hiking into
redwood groves are attractions 18 miles north of Big Sur.

Henry Miller Memorial Library

35 miles south of Carmel. Tel: 831-667-2574; web: www.henrymiller.org.
Open Wed–Sun 1100–1700. Admission: free.

Miller's secretary Emil White founded the library, which
evolved into an alfresco sculpture gallery and a bookstore,
a paean to the iconoclastic author.

Julia Pfeiffer Burns State Park

12 miles south of Pfeiffer Big Sur SP.
Web: http://www.cal-parks.ca.gov/DISTRICTS/monterey/jpbsp.htm.

From December to January and from March to April, the
Overlook Trail is a prime spot for watching grey whales
migrating between Baja California and Alaska.

Pfeiffer-Big Sur State Park

26 miles south of Carmel.
Web: http://www.cal-parks.ca.gov/DISTRICTS/monterey/pbssp.htm.

The popular park has a lodge, cabins, camping and a
grocery store amidst loop hiking trails through redwood,
conifer, cottonwood and maple forest.

Point Sur State Historic Park

15 miles south of Carmel.
Web: http://www.cal-parks.ca.gov/DISTRICTS/monterey/psshp.htm.
Open Mon, Wed, Sat–Sun for guided tours.

Point Sur rock sits offshore with an active lighthouse set
361ft above the water.

Tourist information

Big Sur Chamber of Commerce: *Tel: 831-667-2100; web: www.bigsurcalifornia.org.*
Big Sur Multi-Agency Station: *1/2-mile south of Pfeiffer-Big Sur SP. Tel: 831-667-
2315; web: www.cal-parks.ca.gov/DISTRICTS/monterey. Open daily 0800–1800
summer, to 1700 winter. Fee for access to and camping in state parks and beaches.*

Carmel

Carmel Visitors Center, San Carlos, between 5th and 6th Sts.
Tel: 800-550-4333. Open Mon–Fri 0800–1700.

Carmel's delights are divided between the quaint cottage-style upmarket shops and art/photography galleries along and near Ocean Avenue, its one-of-a-kind homes, the lovely Carmel Beach strand, a California mission and scenic Point Lobos.

Mission San Carlos Borromeo del Rio Carmelo

2080 Rio Rd. Tel: 831-624-3600; web: www.carmelmission.org.
Open Mon–Sat 0930–1630, Sun 1030–1630. Admission: free.

Mission founder Fra Junipero Serra is buried in front of the basilica's main altar. The flower-filled courtyard and fountain were typical of Spanish-era missions. A museum preserves Serra's quarters, the mission kitchen, parlour and library. See also **La Purisima Mission State Historic Park**: a restored adobe mission recalls Spanish conversion when Indians worked the land and assisted friars in leather tanning, animal husbandry and in tending an extensive mission herb garden (*2295 Purisima Rd, Lompoc; tel: 805-733-3713; web: http://www.cal-parks.ca.gov/DISTRICTS/channel/lpmshp513.htm; open daily 0900–1700; admission: $*).

Hearst Castle

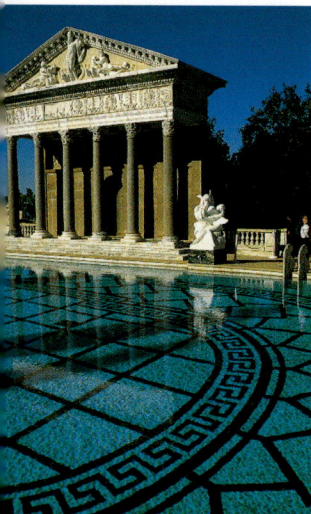

Hearst San Simeon State Historic Monument, 750 Hearst Castle Rd, San Simeon.
Tel: 805-927-2020 or 800-444-4445; web: www.hearstcastle.org. Open daily. Advance bookings essential in summer and recommended all year. Walk-in space may be available midweek mid-Nov–mid-May. Admission: $$.

Newspaper-publishing tycoon William Randolph Hearst engaged architect Julia Morgan to build a hillside castle. Over three decades, 165 rooms were furnished with antiques and interiors from Europe and surrounded with 127 acres of gardens for the pleasure of Hearst and his paramour, actress Marion Davies.

Monterey

Monterey Peninsula Visitors and Convention Bureau: 380 Alvarado St, Monterey. Tel: 831-649-1770; web: www.monterey.com. Open Mon–Fri 0830–1700. Visitor Center: 201 El Estero (Historic Monterey). Open daily 0900–1700.

Little is left of Cannery Row, Steinbeck's raucous sardine cannery waterfront, except the exteriors of buildings, though the Monterey Bay Aquarium building mimics the old processing plants. Shops, restaurants, ice-cream parlours, hotels and an amusement arcade

CHINESE FISHING COLONY, 1850

WAREHOUSE & SHIPPING

with a Looff carousel sit where wooden piers, fishing boats, bars, bordellos and a Chinatown thrived.

Monterey Bay Aquarium

886 Cannery Row. Tel: 831-648-4888 or 800-756-3737; web: www.mbayaq.org. Open daily 0930–1800 mid-June–Labor Day, 1000–1800 rest of year. Admission: $$.

With the 5328-square-mile Monterey Bay Marine Sanctuary outside its back door, the aquarium's habitats include a 335,000-gallon-tank Kelp Forest, with divers feeding fish, Rocky Coast sea otters and Outer Bay sealife – over 300,000 creatures swimming, crawling, floating and reproducing.

Monterey State Historic Park

20 Custom House Plaza. Tel: 831-649-7118; web: www.mbay.net. Open daily 1000–1700 Memorial Day weekend–Labor Day, 1000–1600 rest of year. Admission: free.

Stroll around old Monterey with the *Path of History Walking Tour* guide to elegant adobe buildings. Amongst them, the 1794 Royal Presidio Chapel is still in use and the Larkin House housed the US consul just before the American take-over in 1846.

Nipomo Dunes Preserve

West of Hwy 1 on Hwy 166, W Main St, from Guadalupe, or Oso Flaco Lake exit north of Guadalupe. The Nature Conservancy, 672 Higuera St, San Luis Obispo. Tel: 805-545-9925.

The *Ten Commandments?* In 1923, Cecil B DeMille filmed his Egyptian locations here on 18 miles of dunes where occasional set ruins and Chumash Indian shell middens are visible when the 500ft-high walls of sand shift.

San Luis Obispo

San Luis Obispo Chamber of Commerce, 1039 Chorro St. Tel: 805-781-2777; web: www.VisitSLO.com. Open Tue–Wed 0800–1700, Thur–Fri 0800–2000, Sat 1000–2000, Sun–Mon 1000–1700.

SLO is a gracious city founded by the mission friars a short distance from the Pacific Ocean. California Polytechnic University (Cal Poly) is renowned for its agricultural programmes and a student body which gives a hip, youthful feeling to the tree-lined downtown.

Chewing Gum Alley

Higuera–Marsh Sts between Garden and Broad Sts.

Disgusting, maybe, but the chewing gum along this narrow alley uses a colourful palette to convey current ideas and trends – just don't touch the sticky graffiti.

Mission San Luis Obispo de Tolosa

Chorro and Monterey Sts. Tel: 805-543-6850. Open daily 0900–1600. Museum admission: $.

Gracious **Mission Plaza** park fronts the 1772 mission where conversion of local Native Americans was not accepted as graciously. Chumash artefacts, vestments and photographs make up the museum displays in the former padre's quarters.

Santa Cruz

Beach and Boardwalk

400 Beach St. Tel: 831-423-5590; web: http://www.beachboardwalk.com. Open daily 1100 Memorial Day–Labor Day (closing times vary), Sat–Sun 1100–1900 1 Jan–Memorial Day and Labor Day–30 Nov. Admission: boardwalk free, rides $.

A mile-long strand of beach offers an arcade and 30 rides including the 1924 Giant Dipper roller coaster, a Looff carousel, the spinning Whirlwind, laser tag, miniature golf and virtual reality games. Often the Boardwalk is the only spot on the coast to have sunshine when fog prevails elsewhere.

Santa Cruz Surfing Museum

Ground floor, Mark Abbott Memorial Lighthouse, West Cliff Dr. Tel: 831-429-3429. Open Thur–Mon 1200–1600. Admission: $.

Surfing is so embedded in the culture here that the University of California has a live view camera trained on one of the prime beaches. Museum history traces (heavy!) redwood surfboards to modern state-of-the-art boards, and the 'dudes' who pioneered the sport.

Wilder Ranch State Park

Hwy 1, 2 miles north of Santa Cruz. Tel: 831-426-9703; web: http://www.cal-parks.ca.gov/DISTRICTS/santacruz/wrsp456.htm. Open daily. Admission: $.

Ride a horse, walk or bike in this former dairy ranch along the coast. The golden cliffs and rolling landscape are a surprising contrast to the surfing beaches just south in Santa Cruz.

Tourist information

Santa Cruz County Conference and Visitor Council: *701 Front St. Tel: 831-425-1234 or 800-833-3494; web: www.scccve.org. Open daily.*

Santa Barbara

Santa Barbara, the self-proclaimed American Riviera, has lovingly been called Lotusland, after a lovely garden in its Montecito enclave. A temperate Mediterranean climate merits the tourism bureau's claim of 'Endless Summer', a land where flowering plants grow in profusion.

The city spreads for miles along the coast, sweeping up the flanks of the Santa Ynez Mountains. For decades, it has been *the* place north of Los Angeles where film stars retreat, retire, go to play tennis or watch polo matches. Surfers find 'cool' waves offshore or just south in **Summerland**. Downtown along State St, whitewashed, Spanish-style arcades mimic the old Mission and Rancho days' Presidio, complete with red-tiled roofs and a Red Tile Walking Tour.

El Paseo

800 block of State St near De la Guerra St.

A venerable shopping arcade and courtyard with antique shops and a restaurant occupy the block around the old 1827 De la Guerra adobe. The epitome of elegance has recently been matched by **Paseo Nuevo** (*State and Chapala Sts, from Ortega to Canon Perdido Sts*), with department stores, shops, art galleries, a selection of eateries, the Center Stage Theater, a cinema and live music concerts.

El Presidio de Santa Barbara State Historic Park

100–200 E Canon Perdido St. Tel: 805-965-0093; web: http://www.cal-parks.ca.gov/DISTRICTS/channel/epdsb575.htm. Open daily 1030–1630. Admission: $

When colonising and Christianising Upper California the Spanish built a series of forts; Santa Barbara was the last after San Diego, San Francisco and Monterey. Reconstructed on the 1782 foundations, the Presidio complex includes a recreated Chapel and on-going excavations. Several square blocks around the Presidio are built in the style of old whitewashed adobe homes, complete with second-storey iron balconies.

Mission Santa Barbara

*E Los Olivos and Laguna Sts. Tel: 805-682-4149.
Open daily 0900–1700. Admission: free.*

The 1786 Queen of the Missions was rebuilt after the
major 1925 earthquake to resemble nothing so much
as a pink movie-set façade. A lovely lawn and
municipal rose garden are in front, along a drive
that leads off into the hills by multi-million-dollar
homes in the gracious late-1920s' imitation of
Spanish-Moorish architecture.

17-Mile Drive

Tel: 831-625-8426 or 800-654-9300.

It is worth paying the entrance toll for
this coastal drive. Save the 17-Mile Drive
for a sunny day when the Lone Cypress,
Ghost Tree, Pebble Beach, Cypress Point
and Spyglass Hill Golf Courses, and Bird
Rock show to best advantage against
the golden sand, pebbly beaches and
turquoise blue Pacific waters.

Solvang

Hwy 246. Tel: 805-688-6144 or 800-468-6765.

Danish Solvang is a shopping and bakery opportunity, a
1911 town full of colourful, half-timbered buildings housing
shops, restaurants, and, yes, those bakeries beneath golden
pretzels. Mission Santa Ines and its rose garden survive on
one side; the Santa Ynez Valley is filled with horse ranches,
wineries and even an ostrich farm.

127

Tourist information

Santa Barbara Visitor Information Centers: *Tel: 805-965-3021 or 800-927-
4688; web: www.santabarbara.com.* **Stearn's Wharf**: *vicinity 1 Santa Barbara St
at Cabrillo Blvd. Open Mon–Sat 0900–1700, Sun 1000–1700 May–Sept, Mon–Sat
0900–1600, Sun 1000–1600 Oct–Apr.* **Downtown**: *504 State St. Open Mon–Fri
0900–1700.*

Eating out on the Central Coast

Central Coast dining is often best in the inns and lodges that cater for the posh set. Local, fresh-caught seafood, including ling cod, Petrale sole, red snapper and swordfish as well as farmed abalone is always the best choice, though limited fishing seasons may guide diners to fine steak, rack of lamb, or range-fed chicken. Consult the list of special offerings for what the renowned restaurants want to serve you.

Big Sur

Nepenthe

South of Big Sur Valley. Tel: 831-667-2345. $$. Two restaurants offer a choice of salad and grill or more composed meals at the spot overlooking the Pacific that Orson Welles built for Rita Hayworth and where Burton and Taylor made *The Night of the Iguana*.

Post Ranch Inn's Sierra Mar

Tel: 831-667-2200 or 800-527-2200. $$$. The posh secluded inn serves exquisite dinners, including scallops with ratatouille or quail in peach sauce.

Ventana Inn's Patio Grill

Tel: 831-667-2331 or 800-628-6500. $$$. Like the Post Ranch, Ventana is a well-hidden landmark with dining above the ocean, offering delicate grilled *ahi* (tuna) and other seafood.

Carmel area

The Inn at Spanish Bay and The Lodge at Pebble Beach

17-mile Drive, Pebble Beach. Tel: 831-647-7500 or 800-654-9300. $$$. Two famous hotels and their restaurants offer a choice from **Roy's** East–West fusion menu at Spanish Bay to the **Stillwater Bar & Grill** raw (seafood) bar overlooking the famous 18th hole of the Pebble Beach Golf Links.

Mediterranean Market

Ocean Ave at Mission St. Tel: 831-624-2022. $. Excellent sandwiches to take away provide easy picnicking.

Pasqual's

Junipero between 5th and 6th Sts. Tel: 831-624-2200. $. Pictures of jazz musical greats are on the walls for a California–Continental cuisine combination. Note the leopard-print-covered chairs.

Monterey

Montrio

414 Calle Principal. Tel: 831-648-8880. $$$. Here's the spot to dine on free-range chicken, roasted beet salad and *crème brûlée* in a converted firehall.

Stokes Adobe

500 Hartnell St. Tel: 831-373-1110. $$$. Dine in an historic building on *tapas* or a full meal of lavender-infused pork chop or oven-roasted chicken.

San Luis Obispo

Madonna Inn

100 Madonna Rd. Tel: 805-543-3000 or 800-543-9666. $$. With fantasy rooms upstairs and giftshops full of cut glass off the lobby, this inn is a quaint stop for a cheerful, fancy coffee-shop menu close to Hwy 101.

SLO Brewing Company

1119 Garden St. Tel: 805-543-1843. $$. Bright, cheerful, with a lot of wood and glass, this brewpub makes good home brew and, in keeping with university student taste, offers live music at night.

Santa Cruz

Gabriella Café

910 Cedar St. Tel: 831-457-1667. $$. Small, intimate, this downtown restaurant serves colourful dishes that include fresh vegetables done to perfection.

Santa Cruz Brewing Co & Front Street Pub

516 Front St. Tel: 831-429-8838. $–$$. This microbrewery was one of California's pioneers in custom brewing, and serves straightforward sandwiches and salads.

Santa Barbara

El Encanto Hotel

1900 Lasuen Rd. Tel: 805-687-5000 or 800-346-7039. $$$. In the hills above Santa Barbara, this posh spot makes cocktail hour margaritas that match the splendid sunsets.

Citronelle

901 E Cabrillo Blvd. Tel: 805-963-0111. $$$. Celebrity chef Michel Richard's kitchen serves French–California fusion with a view.

" *The one common note of all this country is the haunting presence of the ocean. A faint great sound of breakers follows you high up into the inland canyons; the roar of water dwells in the clean, empty rooms of Monterey as in a shell upon the chimney; go where you will, you have but to pause and listen to hear the voice of the Pacific.* **"**

Robert Louis Stevenson, *The Old Pacific Capital*, **1880**

Central Coast wine

The Central Coast can't claim California's first winery (Mission San Diego probably planted the state's first grapes), but Mission vineyards from Monterey to Santa Barbara have been winning converts since at least the 1790s. San Luis Obispo, San Miguel and Santa Ines were famed throughout the Spanish world for their wine production, fame that has returned in the modern era. Climate gets the credit.

Wine grapes require a peculiar combination of hot, sunny days and cold nights to produce the ideal balance of flavour, sugar and acidity. Too much heat produces table grapes, luscious and sweet, but lacking the acidic backbone that produces fine wine. Too much cold produces sour, almost flavourless grapes that are fit for little but distilling into brandy.

The rugged Coast Range provides dozens of valleys with different combinations of sun and fog, hot and cold to suit almost any wine grape from any part of the world. Monterey and Santa Cruz counties have become favourites for Rhône varieties as well as rich, old-fashioned wines grown by the descendants of

> *Little, if anything, is predictable in the choppy Coastal Ranges, where all depends on the cold sea air being vacuumed inland through gullies and over passes by the great hot updraught in the Central Valley. Sometimes a promising valley . . . a perfect match for Pauillac or Beaune turned out to be a funnel for howling gales on summer afternoons.*

Hugh Johnson, *Vintage: The History of Wine*, 1989

Italian immigrants who brought vines and wine styles with them a century ago. The relatively cool climate tends to produce grapes bursting with intense flavour that translate into equally rich red and white wines.

The **Monterey County Vintners & Growers Association** (*tel: 831-375-9400; web: www.wines.com/monterey*) offer winery touring information. The easiest way to taste the variety is **A Taste of Monterey** (*Cannery Row, Monterey; tel: 831-646-5446*).

San Luis Obispo has two wine areas. At the north end of the county, wineries around Paso Robles produce more red wines than white, thanks to the hotter, sunnier climate slightly inland. For winery touring information, contact the **Paso Robles Vintners and Growers Association** (*tel: 805-239-2463*) or visit the annual **Wine Festival** (*3rd Sat in May, City Park, Spring St between 11th and 12th Sts*).

South of San Luis Obispo, head for the **Edna Valley**, with wineries scattered near Lopez Dr or Hwy 227, near the town of Arroyo Grande. **Edna Valley/Arroyo Grande Valley Vintners** (*tel: 805-541-5868*) have winery maps and touring information. The cool Edna Valley is best known for Chardonnay and other white wines, but warmer inland areas produce award-winning reds.

Santa Barbara wineries are concentrated near Solvang and Mission Santa Ines. **Santa Barbara County Vintners' Association** (*tel: 805-688-0881 or 800-218-0881*) have touring maps and winery information. Most wineries are located along Foxen Canyon Rd, which runs from Los Olivos north towards Santa Maria, and in the Santa Ynez Valley between Solvang, Santa Ynez and Los Olivos. For easy sampling, stop at the **Wine Cask** (*813 Anacapa St, Santa Barbara; tel: 805-966-9463*).

San Diego

Sailboats and ferryboats, navy ships and kayaks skim across glistening, palm tree-lined San Diego Bay. California's second largest city and first European settlement is the tropics-meets-Mexico. Citizens indulge in plenty of outdoor living and playing amidst an economic comeback story still being built in this thriving Southern California metropolis. Beyond the city are golden sandstone cliffs, flower fields and a wild animal park.

SAN DIEGO

BEST OF
San Diego

North

0 ————————— 5 kms

0 ————————— 2 ½ mile

La Jolla
Scene

California Surf
Museum, Oceanside;
Carlsbad Flower Fields;
Stuart Collection

5 San Diego
Wild Animal Park

Mission Gorge Road

Mission
San Diego

5

Mission
Bay

168

San Diego

San Diego River

San Diego

Sea World

8

15

8

Old Town
San Diego

805

Rosecrans Boulevard

San Diego
International
Airport

1 Balboa
Park

209

Star of India/San Diego
Maritime Museum

Horton Plaza

Seaport
Village

Museum of Death

3 Gaslamp Quarter

North
Island

Trolley to
Tijuana

16

5

75

Hotel del
Coronado **4**

San
Diego
Bay

Point
Loma

Silver Strand Blvd

Cabrillo
National
Monument **2**

Point Loma
Lighthouse

PACIFIC
OCEAN

SAN DIEGO

① Balboa Park

San Diego's urban park may be California's loveliest, with gracious buildings from two world expositions, a host of museums and the San Diego Zoo, all within 10 minutes' drive of downtown. **Pages 136–137**

② Cabrillo National Monument

After the Statue of Liberty in New York harbour, this is the US's most-visited national monument, with a statue of San Diego Bay's 1542 Spanish discoverer, a lighthouse, tidepools and sweeping views from the bay to Mexico. **Page 138**

③ Gaslamp Quarter

San Diego's newer old town retains many finely detailed Victorian-era office buildings and is a centre for restaurant dining and music clubs. Horton Plaza provides a wild and colourful venue for shopping and plenty of parking to explore the district. **Page 139**

④ Hotel Del Coronado

The Disney-imitated 'Del' is San Diego's signature 1888 Victorian seaside hotel, a white wedding cake topped with turrets and a red roof. Coronado Island, reached by bridge or ferry, is shared by the US Navy; the Del and residential districts are posh San Diego at its architectural best. **Page 140**

⑤ San Diego Wild Animal Park

Amidst the hills 30 miles north of San Diego, the Zoological Society has combined lush botanical gardens and mostly African animals and birds in a landscape resembling the African savannah. **Page 142**

Getting there and around

San Diego International Airport, better known as Lindbergh Field, is 3 miles north of downtown. **Amtrak** trains arrive at the **Santa Fe Depot** (*1050 Kettner Blvd; tel: 800-872-7245*). San Diego's freeways, particularly I-5 and I-8, clog at rush hour. Public transport works well here, with clean vehicles and good connections; information from **MTS** (*tel: 619-685-4900 or 619-233-3004*). The **Coaster** train serves North San Diego coastal communities; the **San Diego Trolley** (*tel: 619-232-4002*) runs frequently from downtown to the Mexican border.

Balboa Park

Visitors Center in the House of Hospitality, 1549 El Prado.
Tel: 619-239-0512; web: www.balboapark.com/index.html.
Open daily 0900–1600. Park admission: free.

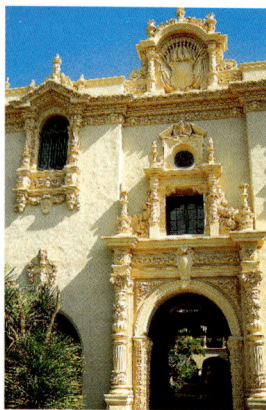

This grand late 19th-century park took its name from **Vasco Nuñez de Balboa** who sighted the Pacific Ocean from Panama in 1513. Balboa Park, the equal of San Francisco's Golden Gate Park, served as a venue for the 1915 Panama-California Exposition and, two decades later, for the 1935 California Pacific International Exposition. Both expos left buildings which combined Spanish, Moorish, baroque and a few fanciful Mayan architectural influences, many of which serve as unique museums. A free **Balboa Park Tram** operates *0900–1715*. **Passport to Balboa Park** (*$*) is a seven-day bargain for the park's 12 museums, though many are free one Tuesday per month.

Museum of Man

California Building, 1350 El Prado. Tel: 619-239-0001; web: www.museumofman.org. Open daily 1000–1630. Admission: $.

Archaeological finds from around the world include mummies from Peru, Egypt and Mexico.

Old Globe Theatre

Simon Edison Center for the Performing Arts, north of the Museum of Man. Tel: 619-239-2255; web. www.oldglobe.org/home.html. Admission: $$.

The Elizabethan-style theatre is famed for its summer season of Shakespeare plays. Two other stages allow for repertory production of classical and modern works.

Other museums

Amongst exhibits and themes at Balboa Park's 10 other museums are Russian icons: **Timken Museum of Art** (*1500 El Prado, Plaza de Panama; tel: 619-239-5548; web: http://www.gort.ucsd.edu.sj.timken*); a world-encompassing collection of folks art and handicrafts: **Mingei International Museum** (*1439 El Prado;*

tel: 619-239-0003; web: www.mingei.org); outdoor abstract sculpture: **San Diego Museum of Art and Sculpture Garden** (*Plaza de Panama; tel: 619-232-7391; web: www.sddt.com/sdma.html*); fine art photography: **Museum of Photographic Arts** (*1649 El Prado; reopens in 2000; tel: 619-238-7559; web: www.mopa.org*); and changing exhibits of classic automobiles: **San Diego Automotive Museum** (*2080 Pan American Plaza; tel: 619-231-2886*). The **Botanical Building** is an open-door conservatory, and the **Spanish Village Arts & Crafts Center** is a grouping of galleries, with artists at work.

San Diego Aerospace Museum

2001 Pan American Plaza. Tel: 619-234-8291; web: www.aerospacemuseum.org. Open daily 1000–1630, free 4th Tue of the month. Admission: $

The doughnut-shaped 1935 Ford Building allows for a unique time-line approach to viewing more than 80 aircraft as you follow the circle through time.

San Diego Zoo

2900 Zoo Dr. Tel: 619-234-3153; web: www.sandiegozoo.com. Open 0900–1600 (closes 1700). Admission: $$$.

Giant Pandas on loan from the People's Republic of China have been the biggest draw for years. Most of the 3900-plus animals and birds live in habitats suited to their needs rather than being caged. At **Flamingo Lagoon**, catch a **brown double-decker bus** for a comprehensive narrated tour or try **Kangaroo Bus Tours**, which stop at eight points.

Cabrillo National Monument

Hwy 209 to 1800 Cabrillo Memorial Dr. Tel: 619-557-5450; web:
www.nps.gov/cabr. Open daily 0900–1715, to 1815 4 July–Labor Day. $.

Above the bay where Juan Rodriguez Cabrillo's ship landed
on 28 September 1542, a **monument** marks Europe's official
first contact with the coastline that later became the US.
The explorer's white statue looks half over his shoulder to
catch the magnificent view, which stretches more than 20
miles south to the mountains along the Mexican border.

The **Old Point Loma Lighthouse** is open for visitors to
explore the 1880s lightkeeper's furnished family quarters
and the light. Check the visitors centre for directions to
the self-guiding mile-long **Bayside** (hiking) **Trail**.

Carlsbad Flower Fields

Carlsbad Convention & Visitors Bureau 400 Carlsbad Village Dr, Carlsbad.
Tel: 760-434-6093 or 800-227-5722; web: www.carlsbadca.org. Open Mon–Fri
0900–1700, Sat 1000–1600, Sun 1000–1500.

Named after the Bohemian spa town, this charming enclave
along North San Diego County's surfing coast has recently
become the site for **LEGOLAND California**, a theme park

more for youngsters enthralled with
the trade-marked building blocks than
for the adult set. In April, acres of
commercially grown ranunculus
bloom at **Carlsbad Ranch** (*east of*
I-5, Palomar Airport Rd and Paseo
del Norte; tel: 760-431-0352; open
daily 0900–dusk late Feb–late May), a
rainbow of colour where visitors are
encouraged to wander and photograph.
Barnstorming Adventures offer open
bi-plane rides over the flower fields
and Pacific Ocean (*6473 Montia Ct,*
Carlsbad; tel: 760-438-7680 or 800-
759-5667; web: www.barnstorming.com;
open daily by advance booking; $$$).

California Surfing Museum

223 N Coast Hwy, Oceanside. Tel: 760-721-6876; web: www.surfmuseum.org. Open Wed–Mon 1000–1600. Admission: $.

From a trendy tandem surfing exhibit to a 155lb redwood board that's too big to move, this is a place where the kahunas, the big-name surfers, stop by to visit and learn about their sport. Outside, down by the Oceanside Pier, as others flock to watch magnificent sunsets over the Pacific, surfers ride pinkish waves silhouetted against the setting sun.

Gaslamp Quarter

Broadway and Harbor Dr, 4th and 6th Aves.

In 1982, San Diego began to refurbish a derelict area of old Victorian buildings which had become a dangerous skid row, lined with relief missions and adult bookstores. A decade later, the district originally developed by speculator Alonzo Horton shone again. Seventy restaurants, antique stores, art galleries, beauty salons and a classic car dealership, Affordable V.I.P. Classics (*851 5th Ave; tel: 619-232-6864*) create a lively district paved with red brick and accented by namesake gaslamps.

Horton Plaza (*Broadway–G St, 1st–4th Aves; tel: 619-238-1596; web: www.hortonplaza.com; open Mon–Sat from 1000, Sun from 1100*) in wild, colourful, geometric architecture at the quarter's west side, has 140 shops, casual and fast-food restaurants, department stores, a cinema and the repertory San Diego Lyceum Theater (*tel: 619-235-8025*).

139

Alonzo Horton

Connecticut-born Horton struck it rich selling ice to miners in the 1849 Gold Rush, profitably sold furniture in San Francisco, then engaged in land speculation in 1867 by buying 960 acres of San Diego waterfront at auction for $265, a steal. He sold land as capital for development of the wharf, a hotel and business blocks, the nucleus of the Gaslamp Quarter, while paying workers in land.

Hotel Del Coronado

1500 Orange Ave, Coronado. Tel: 619-522-8000.
Historic property tours daily: $.

L Frank Baum modelled the Emerald City on the Del, writing six Oz books in a nearby cottage. **Thomas Edison** helped install its electric lights. **Marilyn Monroe**, **Tony Curtis** and **Jack Lemmon** starred alongside it in the 1959 film *Some Like It Hot*. Rooms 3312 and 3502 are both connected with the ghost of Kate Morgan, an 1892 suicide/murder on the beach, whose manifestation varies from footsteps to moving objects and doors and windows that open and close.

La Jolla

La Jolla Town Council, 7734 Herschel Ave. Tel: 619-454-1444.
Open Mon–Fri 0930–1600.

Shop in the upmarket boutiques along **Prospect St** and stop for a drink at the many pavement cafés. The **San Diego Museum of Contemporary Art** (*700 Prospect St; tel: 619-454-3541; web: www.mcasd.org; open Tue–Sat 1000–1700, Wed to 2000, Sun 1200–1700; admission: $*) spans the block between Prospect St and Coast Blvd's mile-long **La Jolla Cove**, which has swimming beneath eroded sandstone cliffs. **La Jolla Cave and Shell Shop** (*1325 Coast Blvd; tel: 619-454-6080; open Mon–Sat 1000–1700, Sun 1100–1700; admission: $*) has a stairway to a secluded cove. The **Salk Institute** (*10010 N Torrey Pines Rd; tel: 619-453-4100 ext 1200; web: www.salk.edu; open Mon–Fri 0830–1700*) has free guided architectural tours (*1100 and 1200*) by reservation.

The **Stephen Birch Aquarium-Museum** (*Scripps Institution of Oceanography; tel: 619-534-3474; web: http://www.aqua.ucsd.edu; open daily 0900–1700; admission: $*) chronicles oceanographic research. The **Stuart Collection** at the **University of California, San Diego** (*9500 Gilman Dr; tel: 619-534-2117*) is a series of eclectic sculptures using landscape and buildings. Amongst them: a huge marble tabletop with poetry, a mosaic snake visible only from the Library windows, and a sculpted forest in a grove of trees.

Mission San Diego de Alcalá

10919 San Diego Mission Rd. Tel: 619-281-8449. Open daily 0900–1700.

California's first mission moved to present-day Mission Valley five years after its 1769 founding. Burned by Native Americans and ruined by earthquake, the rebuilt minor basilica grounds include a small museum, missions' founder Fra Junipero Serra's rectory and lovely gardens.

Museum of Death

548 5th Ave, Gaslamp Quarter. Tel: 619-338-8153. Open daily 1200–2200, Fri–Sat to 2400. Admission: $.

Check your weak stomach and delicate sensibilities before you descend below street level to the city's first mortuary, a straightforward and shocking collection of coffins, serial murderer art and memorabilia, crime scene photos, electric chairs and tools for cadaver preparation. A separate upstairs Freak Farm has live and preserved animals with more than one head or incorrect numbers of limbs.

Land of opportunity

Hungarian aristocrat Agoston Haraszthy arrived in Wisconsin in 1840, 28 years old and ready to make a fortune. When the Gold Rush struck California in 1849, he moved to San Diego, and became county sheriff. He also constructed the county jail, and when the walls didn't hold, was awarded another contract to fortify them. The incorrigible served as a state legislator, US Mint assayer where money 'disappeared', and later built a villa at Buena Vista, where his viticulture techniques pioneered commercial winemaking in California.

Old Town San Diego State Historic Park

2645 San Diego Ave. Tel: 619-220-5422. Open daily 1000–1700. Free.

Amidst souvenir shops, ice-cream sellers, trinket wagons and Mexican restaurants is a fine collection of 1821–72 Mexican/early American adobes on the site of San Diego's original settlement. **Old Town Trolley Tours** conduct motorised narrated tours around the area (*tel: 619-298-8687; web: www.historictours.com/sandiego/trolley.htm; open daily 0900–1600; $$*). Stroll by the **Seeley Stables** for a slide show, tour furnished 1830–49 **La Casa de Estudillo**, watch rangers dip candles or perform other 19th-century chores, stand at attention as a squad of blue-uniformed soldiers presents arms, stop in at the **Colorado House Wells Fargo Museum** or dine at the 1829 **La Casa de Bandini**. Near by, **Heritage Park Row** preserves a group of fine Victorian buildings in a country park.

For a self-guided walking tour, purchase the inexpensive *Old Town San Diego State Historic Park Tour Guide & Brief History*, at Seeley Stables, or take a ranger-led tour.

San Diego Wild Animal Park

15500 San Pasqual Valley Rd, Escondido. Tel: 760-747-8702; web: www.sandiegozoo.org/wap. Open-top safari-style Photo Caravan tours, tel: 760-738-5022. Open daily. Admission: $$.

The wild animals and birds are mostly from South and East Africa, and the setting, resembling a savannah, is stunning. Botanical gardens on the north side are complemented by a self-guiding descent into the almost-literal **Heart of Africa**, where cheetahs loll about, giraffes nibble treetop foliage and large, colourful birds carry on mating displays. Other areas of this not-quite-a-theme-park simulate the Congo River and a Kilimanjaro-area safari walk.

Seaport Village

849 W Harbor Dr. Tel: 619-235-4014; web: www.spvillage.com.
Open 1000–2100, to 2200 June–Aug.

This nautical-themed open-air shopping mall with restaurants has fine views of San Diego Bay, and is a convenient stroll from the modernistic sails of the San Diego Convention Center, the Gaslamp Quarter and Cruise Ship Terminal.

SeaWorld Adventure Park San Diego

Mission Bay. Tel: 619-226-3901; web: www.seaworld.com. Open daily. Admission: $$$. SeaWorld and Universal Studios Hollywood offer a park combo discount.

Famed for its orca (killer) whales, SeaWorld's signature show is **Shamu Adventure**. **Shipwreck Rapids** adds a five-minute, nine-person raft-like ride over an obstacle course to the park's other prime attractions: **Wild Arctic's** simulated helicopter ride to visit beluga whales, polar bears and walrus at the North Pole; Jaws swimming overhead (on the other side of plastic) in **Shark Encounter**; gentle sea cows being rehabilitated in **Manatee Rescue**; and an organised, hands-on, in-the-water **Dolphin Interaction Program** (*tel: 800-380-3202; admission: $$$*).

Star of India and San Diego Maritime Museum

1306 N Harbor Dr. Tel: 619-234-9153; web: www.sdmaritime.com. Open daily 0900–2000, to 2100 in summer.

The *Star of India*'s square rigging is so magnificent that early morning joggers stop in their tracks. Centrepiece of the maritime museum, she is one of three tourable ships. Launched from the Isle of Man in 1863, the *Star of India*, the oldest merchant vessel afloat, still sails San Diego Bay on special occasions. The well-restored 1898 ferry boat, *Berkeley*, saw service on San Francisco Bay. An America's Cup exhibit is below decks. A Scots-built steam yacht, the *Medea*, is alongside the *Berkeley*.

143

Eating out

Restaurants are scattered throughout San Diego, with heavy concentrations in and around Old Town State Historic Park, Horton Plaza and the Gaslamp Quarter. Music clubs lean toward jazz and blues, with lively mariachi *music (guitars, trumpets and singers) in many Mexican restaurants.*

Anthony's Fish Grotto

1360 Harbor Dr (near the Star of India). Tel: 619-232-5103. $$. A local chain of informal fish restaurants plus the more expensive **Star of the Sea Room**, which specialises in local seafood with great harbour views.

Buffalo Joe's

600 5th Ave, Gaslamp Quarter. Tel: 619-236-1616. $$. Try the baby backribs at San Diego's best barbecue restaurant.

Café Coyote

Old Town Esplanade. Tel: 619-291-4695. $$. Great wraps and light meals with Mexican overtones.

Casa de Bandini

2754 Calhoun St, Old Town. Tel: 619-297-8211. $$. Casual Mexican dishes are served in a restored adobe built by an early Presidio commandante. Strolling *mariachi* musicians entertain the diners.

Casa de Pico

2754 Calhoun St, Old Town. Tel: 619-296-3267. $$. Birds could bathe in the giant margaritas, but the outsized drinks and California-Mex dishes lure crowds.

Croce's

5th Ave and F St, Gaslamp Quarter. Tel: 619-233-4355. $$. As popular for music as it is for food, **Top Hat Bar & Grille** has rhythm and blues; **Croce's West** serves Southwest cuisine; and **Croce's Restaurant & Jazz Bar** has jazz and American cuisine.

Edgewater Grill

Seaport Village. Tel: 619-232-7581. $$$. This harbourside restaurant has one of the finest views in all of San Diego.

Hard Rock Café

801 4th Ave, Horton Plaza. Tel: 619-615-7625. $$. This chain has California cuisine and rock 'n' roll memorabilia in the landmark Golden Lion building.

Hornblower

1066 N Harbor Dr. Tel: 619-686-8715. $$$. A fleet of small cruise boats offers regular dinner-dances and Sunday brunches on San Diego Bay.

Karl Strauss Breweries

1157 Columbia St, Downtown; tel: 619-234-2739; and 1044 Wall St, La Jolla; tel: 619-551-2739. $–$$. San Diego's original brewpub produces grilled items and pizzas

SAN DIEGO᠎᠎

145

San Diego backcountry

There's more to San Diego than bay and city delights. This one-day driving loop up the North San Diego Coast and through rugged backcountry spans California from the Mission era, through the decisive battle in American's campaign to conquer California to the modern-day technology race.

Route (120 miles: allow all day)

From **La Jolla**, follow Hwy S21 north to **Torrey Pines State Reserve** and a string of beach towns to **Encinitas, Carlsbad** (*page 138*) and **Oceanside** (*page 139*). Follow Hwy 76 east to **Mission San Luis Rey de Francia**, **Mission San Antonio de Pala** and 11 miles further to the left turn onto Hwy S6 going north to the **Palomar Observatory**.

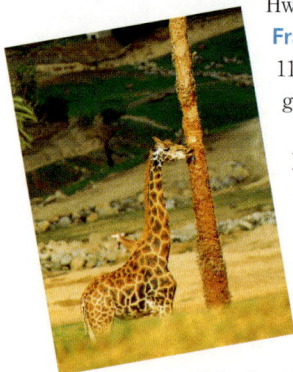

Return south on Hwy S6, turn right on Hwy 76 for 5 miles, then left on Hwy S6 south to Hwy 78 (at **Escondido**). Take Hwy 78 east to **San Diego Wild Animal Park** (*page 142*) and **San Pasqual Battlefield State Historic Park**.

Take San Pasqual Rd back to I-15 and continue south, taking the Hwy 163 exit towards downtown **San Diego**.

Highlights

Torrey Pines State Reserve (*N Torrey Pines Rd; tel: 619-755-2063; admission: $*) protects multi-coloured sandstone cliffs that support the only surviving forest of Torrey pines (*Pinus torreyana*) other than those found on Santa Rosa, one of the Channel Islands in Southern California.

Encinitas is flower heaven. **The Paul Ecke Poinsettia Ranch** (*441 Saxony Rd; tel: 760-753-1134; web: www.ecke.com*) is the largest poinsettia producer in the world. **Quail Botanical Gardens** (*230 Quail Gardens Dr; tel: 760-436-3036; admission: $*) are planted with exotic species from around the world. For quiet, there are the spectacular **Self-Realisation Fellowship Meditation Gardens** (*216 K St; tel: 760-753-1811*), just above a popular surfing beach called 'Swami's'.

Mission San Luis Rey de Francia (*4050 Mission Ave, San Luis Rey; tel: 760-757-3651*). San Luis Rey was one of the richest of the California Missions, with a front wall once graced by 32 arches and cloisters 500ft square. Earthquakes and time have trimmed the complex, but the scalloped white façade with a statue of the royal French saint is still graceful.

Mission San Antonio de Pala (*tel: 760-742-3317*). Built as an *asistencia* (branch) of Mission San Luis Rey in 1816, this is still a parish church. Native American converts painted the chapel wall frescoes.

Palomar Observatory (*tel: 760-742-2119; open daily 0900–1600*) is home to the 200in Hale Telescope, the largest single-mirror telescope in the world. A museum and video detail Palomar discoveries; a viewing platform overlooks the lattice-work giant.

San Pasqual Battlefield State Historic Park (*15808 San Pasqual Valley Rd, Escondido; tel: 760-220-5430*). The possible site of one of the bloodiest battles between American and Mexican troops over California is peaceful. Illustrated signs explain the battle, where both generals claimed ultimate victory (and the larger 1846 war that saw the US take California, Arizona, Colorado and New Mexico from Mexico).

Active California escapes

Most Americans would say that just going to California is escape enough. But if you already live in America's busiest, most active, most outdoors-orientated state, active escape takes on a whole new meaning.

149

Cycling

Cycling is BIG in California. It didn't hurt that Los Angeles native **Greg LeMond** was the first (and so far the only) American to win the *Tour de France* cycle race. A generally mild climate helps, as does stunning scenery within easy cycling of every major city in the state. Most cities have **bike paths** to separate cyclists from motorists, often along scenic corridors such as the beachfront in Los Angeles, Mission Bay in San Diego or Golden Gate Park in San Francisco.

The **Big Sur coast** from Monterey to San Luis Obispo has become a popular biking route. So has **Santa Barbara**, with fine weather and a combination of quiet winery roads, beaches, bike paths and steep gradients through the **Santa Ynez Mountains**.

Mountain bikes are the latest craze. Most ski areas open their ski runs as mountain-bike parks in summer. Parks, national, state and local, are more selective in permitting mountain bikes on trails because of the potential for erosion and collisions between bikers, hikers and equestrians.

Cycles of all descriptions are widely available for hire by the hour, day or week. State law requires all riders, including children, to wear helmets while cycling.

Golf

California thrives on golf. Scarcely a city, town or wide spot in the road doesn't lay claim to at least one course, driving range or putting green, and usually several. Golf is Palm Springs' *raison d'être*, with nearly 100 courses in the Coachella Valley. **Santa Barbara** became Hollywood's first favourite weekend retreat largely on the strength of its golf courses, a rare attraction in California before World War I.

Even Death Valley has its golf course (**Furnace Creek**), kept green with water from underground sources. Three of

the world's most famous courses, **Spyglass Hill**, **Pebble Beach** and the Links at **Spanish Bay**, lie between Monterey and Carmel.

Most, though not all, courses are open to the public, but tee times at popular courses are often booked up weeks in advance during high season. Try for early morning tee times or, better still, plan to play in the off season. Even Palm Springs courses have space during the summer. And if nine holes seem too much, try a round of miniature golf, putting through mazes, trap doors and other obstacles strictly for the fun of it.

Hang-gliding

Who hasn't dreamed of running off a cliff to soar through the air, keeping pace with eagles as they ride the winds? It's called hang-gliding and it can be done almost anywhere with cliffs to jump off and strong upward winds (updrafts) to keep gliders aloft. Lessons are absolutely required unless you want a single very short flight, straight down. Top locations include **Fort Funston**, in the **Golden Gate National Recreation Area** (San Francisco) and **Torrey Pines State Reserve**, north of La Jolla (San Diego).

Hiring hogs
and convertibles

Hot motorcycles have been part of the California mystique at least since 1954. That's when a sloe-eyed Marlon Brando burst upon a small Central Valley town (and the world) astride a Harley-Davidson in *The Wild One*. Harleys – hogs to aficionados – appear to have aged better than Brando, but motorcycles have become a popular way to tour, for a day if not for an entire holiday. Check the telephone book *Yellow Pages* under 'motorcycle rentals'. And if four wheels have more appeal than two, every car-hire company has a selection of convertibles, but book early, especially in Southern California. Supplies are limited, even if the allure of driving with the top down isn't.

Hot-air ballooning

Wine Country (**Napa Sonoma** and **Temecula**) helped turn hot-air ballooning from a genteel pastime for rich eccentrics into a must-see, must-do experience. There's something engaging, almost lunatic, about climbing into a waist-high wicker basket, or gondola, beneath a 150ft balloon filled with nothing more substantial than hot air, then drifting into the skies to wander at the whim of the breezes.

Hot-air balloons seldom soar more than 1000ft above the ground, but the pilot can bob up and down to catch winds in different directions – a jet blast from enormous propane burners mounted above the basket to rise (wear a hat against the heat), allowing the air in the balloon to cool in order to descend. Between burner blasts, the only sounds are the ones drifting up from below. Moving at the same speed as the wind, there's no breeze, no vibration, no sensation of movement as the ground drifts below.

Rock climbing

Rock climbing is the direct descendant of alpine climbing techniques developed in the Alps. But instead of conquering snow- and ice-clad peaks, rock climbers challenge rock faces at more approachable altitudes. The ultimate: climbing a smooth rock wall using nothing more than fingers, toes, elbows and knees.

Yosemite National Park is *the* mecca for rock climbers, dominated by the sheer 3000ft face of **El Capitan** and dozens of less obvious, but more difficult ascents. The Yosemite climbing school attracts students from around the world, rank beginners to ranked experts, to hone their skills. When Yosemite is wreathed in snow, climbers head to the golden sandstone boulders of **Joshua Tree National Park**.

" *You're a long ways off the ground with the fear factor thrown in. It's a workout you can pull off even if you're tired. You can push as hard or as little as you want to see views as you can from no other place.* "

Ken Yager, veteran rock climber with numerous ascents of 3000ft El Capitan in Yosemite National Park, the largest granite extrusion in the world

Rollerblading

Rollerblades (a cross between ice-skates and roller skates, with a row of narrow wheels creating a rolling blade) are faster than roller skates, more manoeuvrable, more graceful and, yes, easier to fall off. Blades are also hugely popular, especially in **Balboa Park** (San Diego), **Golden Gate Park** (San Francisco) and beachfront bike paths throughout Los Angeles. As exercise, they're easier on the knees and ankles than running and more portable than a bicycle. Street hockey on rollerblades is more like ice hockey than field hockey, and rollerbladers can weave in and out of bicycle traffic as easily as cyclists weave amongst cars on busy city streets.

Sailing

Sailing is enormously popular in California, especially on **San Francisco Bay** and anywhere from Santa Barbara south. San Francisco is one of the most challenging bays in the world to sail, thanks to constantly shifting winds, ferocious tides and fogs that can shroud the Golden Gate in minutes.

Southern California is more sailing for the fun of it, wandering up and down the coast in warm weather and consistent winds. Cruise among the **Channel Islands** or sail out to Avalon, the chief harbour on **Catalina Island**, like Errol Flynn and fellow Hollywood stars of the 1930s and 1940s. Boats can be hired in every port, from tiny one-person Sunfish to crewed yachts.

153

Scuba diving

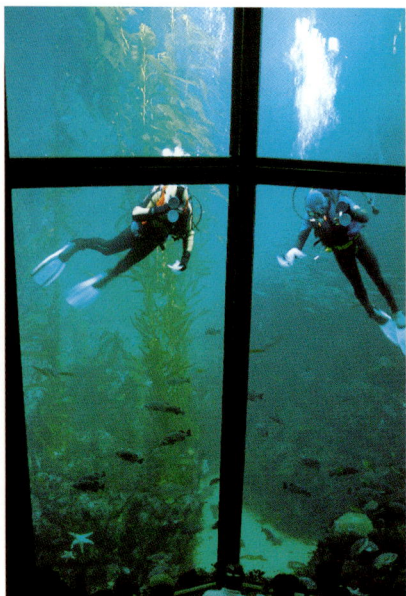

Underwater sightseeing was born in France and developed in Southern California. From Santa Barbara to San Diego, Southern California is one of the most popular cold-water diving areas in the world. Generally mild weather helps, and relatively warm water, but underwater scenery and marine life are the real stars.

Coastal coves are alive with fish, while vast forests of kelp wave in the gentle currents just off shore. The Channel Islands are a marine sanctuary, filled with seals, sea lions and more fish than any aquarium can collect. For the more adventurous, there are wrecks, artificial reefs and dives that seek out sharks.

The **Monterey Bay** area, including **Point Lobos**, is the hot dive spot in Northern California. Sea otters and seals play in the kelp forests, while schools of fish twist between the thick stems like immense flocks of birds.

Winter is the best season for diving, when lower temperatures bring clearer water. Dive boats offer regular trips and offer complete equipment for hire. All divers *must* have a certification card (**C card**) from a recognised agency; operators may also ask about experience and ask to inspect your log book.

"People have become impressed with the diversity of life in the rain forests. But there's nothing like the diversity of life in the sea. Nowhere else do you find this sweep of life that you can find a few feet from any shore. That's what lured me into the ocean. All those critters! It still does."

Sylvia Earle, marine biologist, former Chief Scientist for the US National Oceanographic and Atmospheric Administration, world record for deepest untethered descent, 1250ft, in Hawaii

Skiing

The 1960 Winter Olympic Games were held at **Squaw Valley**, near Lake Tahoe, and California skiing has never been the same. The Sierra Nevada is peppered with alpine and Nordic ski areas, some strictly local, some world-class and most somewhere in between. The ski season generally runs from late November at least through Easter, sometimes into May. Expect crowds at weekends and nearly empty slopes midweek except during school holidays. Always carry tyre chains and allow for slow, tortuous return drives to urban areas on Sunday afternoons. Northern Californians head for **Lake Tahoe**, ringed by jagged Sierra Nevada peaks and ski mountains. At the south end of Lake Tahoe, Heavenly (ski resort) offers mouth-dropping views into Lake Tahoe. **Squaw Valley** is the posh mountain. **North Star** and other north Lake Tahoe resorts cater more for families.

Central California drives to **Yosemite National Park** and **Badger Pass**, the oldest developed ski area in California and still among the most relaxed. Los Angeles heads for **Mammoth Mountain**, a massive resort on the eastern side of the Sierra Nevada.

Spas

A spa escape doesn't have to be active, though a growing number of spas devote as much attention to movement and exercise as they do to massage, aromatherapy and other passive treatments. Either way, spa possibilities have expanded well beyond the original handful in **Calistoga**, **Carlsbad** and **Hollywood**.

It wasn't long ago that treatments ran a rather narrow gamut from mud baths to steam baths, wet wraps and massage. Today, the choices are as wide as the imagination: grape wraps in **Wine Country**, thalassotherapy in **the desert**, Boltair Beds, weight lifting, crystal massages, sensory deprivation, dawn hikes, pyramid trances, high protein diets, no protein diets and a choice of American Indian, East Indian and West Indian high colonics.

Surfing

Surfers Rule! would have been the ultimate California graffiti from the early 1960s, but surfers were too busy surfing to scrawl slogans or to do much else. So was the rest of California, at least that huge population bulge that was somewhere beyond puberty and before marriage. Surfing wasn't just a sport, it was a way of life that took the world by storm.

The Beach Boys rode a wave of music built on surfing, even though the group's chief song writer, Brian Wilson, was terrified of the ocean and absolutely refused to set foot on a board. Sun-streaked hair and deep suntans became the *sine qua non* of adolescence and beyond. They still are.

> " Let's go surfin' now
> Everybody's learnin' how
> Come on a surfin' safari with me. "
>
> **The Beach Boys, *Surfin' Safari*, 1962**

Surfrider Beach, near Malibu, is generally acknowledged as the home of surfing in California, but surfers line up in the water up and down the state, waiting for that perfect wave to come rolling in from the vast Pacific Ocean. Hot spots: **Stinson Beach**, in Marin County; **Maverick**'s mountainous winter waves near Half Moon Bay; **Santa Cruz**; **Santa Barbara**; **Huntington Beach**; **Oceanside**; and **San Clemente**. Surf shops hire out boards and wetsuits.

Tennis

California may have more tennis camps – and tennis courts – than any other state. Even Palm Springs, the golf capital of the state, is replete with tennis courts, tennis tournaments and tennis stars. Most municipalities have their own courts, nearly all are free and most are empty except at weekends.

Whale watching

The state is best known for the annual migration of grey whales: southbound from Alaska in autumn to calving grounds in Baja California and the Sea of Cortez; back north to feeding grounds in Alaska each spring. The spouting leviathans are easily visible from much of the shoreline along Southern California and again from Half Moon Bay and the Point Reyes Lighthouse

Humpback whales also migrate along the California shore, though they tend to stay further out and are rarely visible from land. Blue whales and other species also haunt the deep waters just off the coast.

The easiest way to see whales is from a whale-watching cruise, sailing from most ports during the autumn–spring season. Ships aren't allowed to chase whales, but captains try to guess where the huge mammals are headed and wait for them to arrive. No guarantees, but sightings are more common than not, especially in Northern California, which has less coastal traffic for whales to avoid by swimming further from shore.

White water

California doesn't have extended stretches of white water such as the Grand Canyon in Arizona, but every river flowing west from the Sierra Nevada has its aficionados: the American, Feather, Klamath, Merced, Trinity, Tuolumne and other rivers offer conditions from smooth water to near-suicidal Class 6 rapids for canoeists, kayakers and rafters.

If rapids seem on the tame side, the entire coastline is open for ocean kayaking. Some kayakers hug the rocky coastline, depending on skill, the rhythm of the waves and *Mad Max*-style body armour for protection. Other sea kayakers take to calmer waters, exploring protected areas like Elkhorn Slough, Monterey Bay and Morro Bay

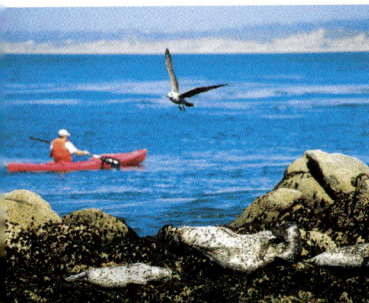

157

The nitty gritty

There's no lack of outdoor adventures in California, but advance information and bookings can be sketchy, especially from outside the state.

For general information and tips, start with the **California State Department of Tourism, California Division of Tourism** (*801 K St, Ste 1600, Sacramento; tel: 916-322-2881 or 800-863-2543; web: http://www.gocalif.ca.gov*).

For activities at **national parks**, monuments and seashores, contact **National Parks of the West** (*Western Region Information Center, Fort Mason, Bldg 201, San Francisco; tel: 415-556-0560; web: http://www.nps.gov*). For **state** parks and beaches, try the **State of California Department of Parks and Recreation** (*PO Box 942896, Sacramento; tel: 916-653-6995 or 800-444-7275; web: http://www.cal-parks.ca.gov*).

California's mild climate makes **cycling** good all year except in the mountains, when winter snow is a concern. The best months are Oct–Nov, when winds are calmer, the most difficult Mar–Apr, when spring breezes gust up to 40mph. Cycles can be hired by the day or the hour almost anywhere. For organised cycle tours, try **Backroads Bicycle Tours** (*801 Cedar St, Berkeley; tel: 510-527-1555 or 800-462-2848; web: http://www.backroads.com; $$*).

The single best source for **hang-gliding**, paragliding and parachuting operators and lessons is the **United States Hang Gliding Association** (*tel: 719-632-8300; web: http://www.ushga.org*).

The California coast is a magnet for **scuba divers**. Nearly every coastal city, town and hamlet has at least one dive shop or boat operator offering local diving, but most shops are concentrated in two areas: San Francisco to Monterey, and Santa Barbara to San Diego. Dive operators are affiliated with at least one, sometimes both, of the two largest scuba-diving certification agencies in the US, NAUI and PADI. For dive-shop locations, contact **NAUI** (*9942 Currie Davis Dr, Ste H, Tampa; tel: 813-628-6284 or 800-553-6284; web:*

http://www.naui.org) or **PADI** (*30151 Tomas St, Rancho Santa Margarita; tel: 949-858-7234 or 800-729-7234; web: http://www.padi.com*). Advance booking is essential, full hire gear is available.

Surf shops are nearly as ubiquitous as scuba shops, fine for surfers, bummer for Barneys, one of the more polite terms for surfer wannabes. The best way to leave barneyhood behind is a five-day stint (*Apr–Sept*) at **Surf Camp** (*San Clemente; tel: 949-361-9283; e-mail surfcamp@aol.com; $$$*). Board, wetsuit, camping and meals included. Surfing museums are an easy way to check out the action without getting wet. **Huntington Beach International Surfing Museum** (*411 Olive Ave, Huntington Beach; tel: 714-960-3483. $*). **California Surfing Museum** (*223 N Coast Hwy, Oceanside; tel: 760-721-6876. $*). **Santa Cruz Surfing Museum** (*West Cliff Dr, Santa Cruz; tel: 831-429-3429. $*). **Waveline** (*154 E Thompson Blvd, Ventura; tel: 805-652-2201*).

There are innumerable river, rafting and kayaking tours available up and down the state. See area listings in the previous chapters for local suggestions. For white-water river rafting state-wide, contact **O.A.R.S.** (*tel: 209-736-4677 or 800-346-6277; web: http://www.oars.com/index.html; $$*). Most California river trips run Apr–Oct, but water levels can run extremely low late in the season. Advance booking required.

" *Despite strips and pockets where the cars are jammed and the housing is crowded, 90% of the land here is wild, unsettled and beautiful. The [San Francisco] Bay Area has 125 significant parks, 5000 miles of hiking trails, 50 lakes and a bay dotted with islands. The state has 20 million acres of national forest, 17.5 million acres of land under the Bureau of Land Management, 373 drive-to lakes, 483 significant lakes you can hike to and 185 streams, each with many tributaries. The land has no limit – and neither do you.* "

Tom Stienstra, introduction to
*Outdoor Getaway Guide:
Northern California*

Golden heroes

California likes to appropriate the best and ignore the rest in any field. Here's a selection of California-proclaimed sports heroes, some of whom were actually born here.

Joe DiMaggio rose from the sandlots of San Francisco to become a legend in American baseball and the envy of every American male as the one-time husband of Marilyn Monroe. 'Joltin Joe', as DiMaggio was called for his hitting abilities, set records in the 1940s that have never been broken. By the time of his death in 1999, DiMaggio was cultural hero as much as sports hero, the subject of songs, plays and films extolling his unassuming manner as well as his fluid, graceful movements on the baseball field. DiMaggio went out of his way to avoid publicity and attention, which earned him a reputation as the most dignified hero in modern American history.

> " *It's* déjà vu *all over again.* "
>
> **Yogi Berra, legendary baseball catcher and coach**

Long Beach-born **Billie Jean King** was setting tennis records long before she trounced self-proclaimed male chauvinist pig Bobby Riggs in straight sets in 1973. King was the first female athlete in history to win more than $100,000 in a single season and the first woman to be named 'Sportsperson of the Year' by *Sports Illustrated* magazine (1972). King created the first successful women's professional tennis tour (1970) and won 20 Wimbledon titles, 13 US Open titles, the French Open, the Australian Open and 29 Virginia Slims singles titles. Not a bad record for a girl who told her mother after an initial tennis lesson at the age of 11 that 'I want to play tennis forever. I'm going to be Number One in the world'.

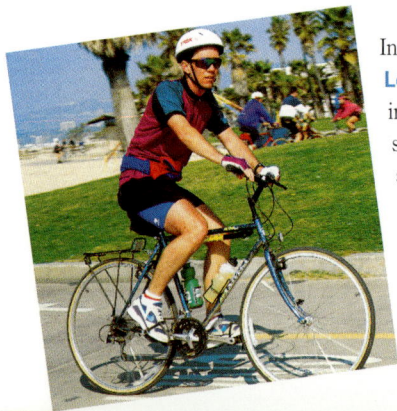

In the summer of 1989, cyclist **Greg LeMond** rode to an 8-second victory in the *Tour de France*, the largest sporting event on earth. It was the second time the Los Angeles native had taken the 2000-mile race, and the toughest of his three *Tour de France* victories.

A bizarre series of accidents – a broken wrist, an appendectomy and a hunting accident – had threatened to cut his career short. Instead, LeMond returned to the Sierra Nevada mountain roads where he had trained for his first *Tour de France* victory in 1986, the first time an American had won the French title. As he rebuilt his physical strength, LeMond honed training techniques and equipment that have become standard: heart-rate monitors, aerodynamic helmets, protective eye-wear, wind-tunnel testing, aeroframes and more.

Tiger Woods exploded into professional golf in 1997, winning the Masters Tournament by a record margin of 12 strokes, the youngest winner (aged 21) in tournament history. That was on top of being the youngest-ever winner of the US Junior Amateur Championship (aged 15, in 1991) and the only person to win the title three times. Woods got an early start in golf, putting with Bob Hope on US television when he was 2 years old. He hit the pages of *Golf Digest* at the age of 5, a year too young to enter elementary school in Cypress, near Los Angeles.

Kristi Yamaguchi started ice-skating in Fremont (near San Francisco) at the age of 6 as physical therapy. Fifteen years later, in 1992, she won gold medals at the Olympic Winter Games, the World Championship and the US Championship.

In between, Yamaguchi was one of the most successful amateur ice-skaters in modern history, with a string of international championships for single and pairs skating (with Rudy Galindo) stretching back to 1988. Yamaguchi turned professional in 1993, touring with *Stars On Ice* and working with the Make-A-Wish Foundation for terminally ill children.

Lifestyles

Shopping, eating, children and nightlife in California

163

Shopping

*Shopping in California is not for the faint of heart – or for the faint of wallet. Buying is a full contact sport, whether you're pushing credit cards to the limit along **Rodeo Drive** in Beverly Hills, checking out the latest avant-garde artiste in SOMA (San Francisco) or simply stocking up on theme park souvenirs from around the state.*

It's not that shopping opportunities are few or far between. Born-to-it shoppers can spend an entire holiday flitting from mall to mall without attracting the slightest bit of attention amidst the hordes of indigenous mall rats. Shopping malls, in fact, are only peripherally about shopping. Visitor guides tout the likes of **Shoreline Village** (San Diego), **The Block at Orange** (City of Orange), **Fashion Island** (Newport Beach), **Metreon** (San Francisco) and dozens of other shopping malls as destinations in their own right, not just places to buy things. The guides are right. The mall has become the latest entertainment venue, a place to see and be seen as much as it is a place to eat out, see the latest hit film or actually make a purchase.

As for what to buy, there's precious little to be had in California that isn't readily available in London, Hong Kong, Cape Town or Sydney. But like so much of California, shopping is more about the experience of buying something than it is about the thing itself. Two good guides: *Born to Shop Los Angeles: The Insiders Guide to Name-Brand, Designer, and Bargain Shopping*, by Suzy Gershman and Judith Thomas; and *Bargain Hunting in the Bay Area*, by Sally Socolich (1997, 12th edn, Chronicle Books).

Arts and crafts fairs and **street fairs** can be great places to browse away an idle afternoon and pick up

enough hand-made goodies to fill an oversized suitcase. Perennial favourites include stained-glass creations, ceramics, blown glass,

woodwork, jewellery and leatherwork, but offerings run the gamut from outsized lawn furniture to photographs, freshly baked breads, garden plants, puzzles and refrigerator magnets. Larger fairs are listed in the California Department of Tourism booklet *California Celebrations*, or check local newspapers. The most popular season is spring–autumn, especially Memorial Day weekend (last weekend in May), 4 July and Labor Day weekend (first weekend in Sept). Many sellers accept credit cards.

Brand-name stores are the latest retail craze. From Disney (The Disney Store) to FAO Schwarz (toys) Nike (Niketown) and Sony (The Sony Store), brand-name marketers are trying to leverage their brands to raise consumer awareness and boost sales. Forget about bargains. In fact, brand-name products may be *more* expensive in the brand's own store than anywhere else, but as theatre, they're hard to beat. Credit cards are happily accepted.

Discount stores offer a good-value combination of price plus quality that appeals to just about everyone in California, from the film stars and fashion models who hawk their own brands to the millions of shoppers who snap them up. Kmart, Target and Walmart are the major discount chains. Look for sale advertisements in Sunday newspapers.

Factory outlets are a fantasy land touched with a glimmer of reality. The fantasy is a store (more often an entire mall) that sells nothing but brand-name factory over-runs and slightly imperfect merchandise for fabulous savings. The reality: brand-name factory over-runs or slightly imperfect (chipped, dented, mismatched seams) merchandise for savings that might beat sales prices at discount department stores. But you get to spend time and money in an adult theme park dedicated to the proposition that shopping is *fun*!

165

Factory outlet shopping is easy to find. Tourist brochures up and down the state advertise the nearest, the biggest, the newest outlet shopping opportunity, usually with easy freeway access and acres of free parking. Credit cards are almost always accepted.

Farmers markets are a growing institution. Originally created for small farmers to sell fresh produce directly to urban consumers, many farmers markets have grown to include local preserves, honey, artisans and handicrafts sellers. Markets are also an easy stop for picnic supplies. Expect to pay cash.

Flea markets are garage sales writ large, formalised and institutionalised to the point that sellers nearly always collect state sales tax. Merchandise is generally legitimate, though sellers sometimes drop broad hints about bargains on (stolen) goods that 'fell off the back of the lorry'. Look for clothing, costume jewellery, handicrafts and bric-à-brac. Some merchants accept credit cards.

Food festivals and **music festivals**, especially celebrations held out of doors, almost always include shopping opportunities. Food and music are obvious products, but expect selections of tie-dye clothing, logo wear and handicrafts as well. Some sellers take credit cards, but cash is preferred for all but large purchases.

Garage sales are a weekend staple in almost every residential neighbourhood. The idea is to clean out the odds and ends that collect in garages, back cupboards, spare rooms and attics over the years, on the theory that one person's junk is someone else's treasure. Items on offer vary wildly, from outmoded record players and broken-down furniture to jewellery and consumer electronics. Most garage sales are family affairs, but neighbours occasionally pool their goods and efforts to lure more buyers. And unlike most venues, discreet bargaining is expected. Churches, Scout troops and social organisations sometimes raise funds by selling similar merchandise at **rummage sales**. Cash only, but individual purchases are usually small.

Museum shops are frequently overlooked as shopping opportunities. There are no bargains to be had, but the quality is extremely high. Pick your shop based on the museum and its current exhibitions: fossils and dinosaur toys at a natural history museum, Egyptian reproductions in conjunction with an Egyptology exhibition, modern art and reproductions at a modern art museum. Museum shops are particularly good for jewellery and similar small items. Credit cards accepted.

Open studios are the latest wrinkle in the California art world. In an effort to make art more accessible (and to boost sales), local artists open their studios to the public on specific days (usually weekends), offering demonstrations, personal explanations and slightly lower prices on selected works. Cash and credit cards accepted.

Renaissance 'faires' offer a glimpse into England's past, or at least England the way California imagines it should have been. The theme is lusty Elizabethan, complete with bawdy ballads, *double entendres* in iambic pentameters, knights in shining armour and shop, shop, shop 'til you drop. The wares are all vaguely 16th century in look or inspiration, from pewter goblets and basket-hilt swords to lavender wands and birch brooms, but merchants are more than willing to accept such modern innovations as credit cards.

Theme parks depend heavily on shopping profits; don't expect to escape without weaving your way through row after row of souvenirs, all tied to the park theme. If you absolutely have to have the Mickey Mouse ears or the Yosemite Sam hat, the theme park is as good a place as any to buy. The park probably offers the best selection of sizes, colours and variety you'll find. And while similar items are available at shops outside the park, prices are almost identical because of product licensing and marketing restrictions. Cash is king, but credit cards run a close second.

167

Eating out

California restaurants are consciously conceived as theatre, complete with troupes of would-be actors masquerading as servers, presenting works of edible art under the watchful eyes of patrons who act the part of an audience that may – or may not – be willing to suspend their disbelief. Smoking is a crime, tipping all but mandatory and service an unpredictable combination of fey, obsequious, challenging and informative.

Blame history. Every cuisine that has passed through California has left its imprint, starting with the Spanish and Mexican padres, soldiers and settlers. Those first immigrants brought a taste for onions, garlic, sugar, chillies, corn (maize), beans, beef, tomatoes and wine. The Native American diet of wild greens, acorns, seeds, fish and game didn't stand a chance.

Two centuries of non-stop **immigration** from every corner of the globe has brought nearly every possible comestible to California and every possible way to prepare it. A piece of fish could be served raw, as sashimi, a Japanese delicacy, cooked in a rich French *bouillabaisse*, deep fried for fish and chips, or preserved in lye as *lutefisk*, a Scandinavian delight.

In a state where Mexican, Chinese, Japanese, Italian and Thai restaurants are as mainstream as McDonalds

and Kentucky Fried Chicken, it's hard to call anything 'traditional Californian'. All-American favourites like hamburgers with catsup – a spicy tomato sauce that originated in Malaysia – have given way to hamburgers with *salsa*, a Mexican sauce of tomatoes, onions, peppers, chillies, cilantro and vinegar. Chopsticks are second nature in many families, including the ones whose ancestors hailed from Prague, Mexicali and Hooting-on-Rye rather than Kyoto, Shanghai or Seoul.

There *are* a few standards, including **meal times**: breakfast 0700–0900, lunch, the midday meal, around

noon, and dinner, the main meal of the day, 1800–2000. Finding late-night snacks can be difficult. Some fast-food outlets are open until midnight, some petrol stations have convenience stores that sell food and chain restaurants near freeways are usually open 24 hours.

Smoking is against the law in all California restaurants and bars. Restaurants don't add service charges, but **tips** are expected, 15–20 per cent of the bill before taxes – waiters/ waitresses are poorly paid in the expectation of tips. The one place you don't need to tip is fast-food outlets, where you order and pick food up from the counter yourself. Fast food is everywhere, from airports and theme parks to hospitals and shopping malls.

Rabid carnivores will have an easier time than rabid vegans, though most towns (and restaurants) offer some sort of vegetarian alternative. If you're in the mood for ethnic food, usually a good choice, start with ethnic neighbourhoods. You're more likely to find a tasty Japanese restaurant in Japantown (San Francisco) or Little Tokyo (Los Angeles) than in a district that is largely Hispanic or Russian, but not always. Ask for suggestions at your hotel. Local alternative newspapers tend to feature practical eating out at smaller, less expensive restaurants.

Fast-food restaurants seldom serve beer, wine or spirits. Some moderate-price chains serve alcohol, although many do not. Most ethnic restaurants serve beer and wine, more expensive restaurants have a full bar. Brew pubs, restaurants which brew their own beer, usually serve wine in addition to beer.

California restaurants are best known for an ever-evolving fusion of ethnic traditions that has come to be called '**California Cuisine**'. Sometimes successful, sometimes not, California Cuisine is an eclectic

169

mixture of fresh, preferably local, ingredients that blends the cooking styles, flavours and foods that have collided here. The basic currents combine French, Italian, Mexican, Chinese, Thai and Japanese influences. The combinations can be as familiar as a grilled steak with garlic mashed potatoes or as unexpected as crispy smoked Chinese duck in a smouldering red *molé* sauce from Mexico atop Moroccan couscous. There is also a strong undercurrent of 'traditional' American cooking. This 'comfort food' recreates family-style dishes such as meatloaf, mashed potatoes, beef stew, hearty soups and apple pie.

Comfort food or California Cuisine, the rule of thumb is simple: fresh is good; anything from a tin or a bottle (except wine, mustard or hot pepper sauce) is bad.

Californians are demanding ever more dew-fresh greens, baby vegetables, fresh fish, local meat and poultry, speciality cheeses and similar items. Growing demand has sparked a renaissance in small-scale and **organic** farming up and down the state. Hand-made brie, camembert, goat and sheep cheeses command the same high prices as their imported counterparts in local speciality markets – sometimes even higher. Duck and lamb from Sonoma County is as revered as authentic *foie gras* from France, which is indistinguishable from local livers.

Credit for the boom in California Cuisine generally goes to **Alice**

Waters, whose **Chez Panisse** (*1517 Shattuck Ave, Berkeley; tel: 510-548-5525; $$$*) has been touted as a temple of Epicurean delight for a quarter-century. The menu is set, the prices sky-high and the limited seating booked up weeks in advance, but **foodies**, as food fanatics call themselves, are so enraptured with the experience that the food hardly matters.

Michael McCarty launched a similar Californicised version of classical French cuisine in Southern California. **Michael's** (*1147 Third St, Santa Monica; tel: 310-451-0843; $$$*) is just as trendy as Chez Panisse, just as pricey and just as hard to get into.

Then came **Wolfgang Puck**, who had a flare for promotion that would do any cinema studio proud. His **Spago Hollywood** (*1114 Horn Ave, West Hollywood; tel: 310-652-3706; $$$*) lured as many paparazzi and newspaper headlines as stars. The new style, essentially classical French dishes with ingredients and fillips from Asia and Mexico, took off. California Cuisine shares space with French, Chinese, Italian, Thai, Russian and a polyglot stew of ethnic cookery around the world.

Fortunately, California Cuisine hasn't taken over California. Traditional breads are making a come-back, including sourdough-style bread that is still widely sold in San Francisco. It's still possible to find home-grown dishes such as **Hangtown Fry**, which hails from

a Gold Rush settlement called Hangtown (now Placerville), for its favourite form of justice. The original fry was a bar meal made up of whatever was handy, usually a mix of potatoes, oysters and sausage, fried and scrambled with eggs.

The latest addition to California menus is the **wrap**. It's a *burrito* by any other name, originally a large *tortilla*, a flat, unleavened round made of corn or wheat flour, folded around meat, beans and rice. What started as an easy-to-carry meal that Mexican farm workers took to the fields has gone international. The basic wrappers haven't changed

much, but the fillings can be as traditional as *carnitas*, Mexican-style roast pork, or as unexpected as jerked chicken (Jamaica), *sashimi* (raw fish), beef tartare, spinach salad or fresh fruit spiked with lime juice, salt and hot chillies.

Want to make your own meal? Fast-food restaurants always offer take-aways, as do most ethnic restaurants. Larger supermarkets have bakeries and deli sections with prepared sandwiches and other items to take away. Sandwiches from delicatessens, or delis, are usually far tastier and only slightly more expensive than supermarket sandwiches.

California with children

Think of California as an enormous theme park, loaded with everything that kids – and their parents – love most about holidays. Mountains to climb, tidepools to explore, beaches, cities, new foods, museums, sailing ships, abandoned prisons, living history, cable cars, Mickey Mouse, desert dunes and thrilling water slides: California has them all.

The problem is picking the best and leaving the rest, the best for kids, that is. Children like nothing better than to work themselves into a frenzy of anticipation, then have the reality come to life with even more excitement than they had imagined. The best way to ensure that the kids (and you) have a good time is to make them part of the planning.

If they're old enough, give them this book, along with every brochure you've managed to collect, and let them start picking out favourites they *absolutely* have to see.

Need more information about, say, **Knott's Berry Farm** (*page 27*), bicycling on **Angel Island** (*page 56*) or the **Santa Cruz Beach Boardwalk** (*page 125*). Let the kids write or e-mail for more information. Once it arrives, have them show *you* just what it is that is going to make that particular visit the most thrilling part of the whole holiday.

Even if the children are too young to write for more information themselves, encourage them to tell you what they want to know more about. A little judicious prompting wouldn't hurt. If Barney the dinosaur is a big hit at home, think about talking up the oversized outdoor dinos at **La Brea Tar Pits in Los Angeles** (*page 28*) or the dino skeletons on display at the **Natural History Museum** in the **California Academy of Sciences** in San Francisco (*pages 44–45*).

Need more suggestions? Try *Weekend Adventures in Northern California*, by Carole Terwilliger Meyers (Carousel Press, Berkeley). Globe-Pequot Press has two California guides for children (and their parents): *Fun With The Family in Northern California*, by Karen Misuraca, and *Fun with the Family in Southern California*, by Laura Kath and Pamela Lechtman.

Life on the road can be tough on, and with, children. Distances are vast in California, and so is the time on the road. A traditional pastime for American families, who face long drives every holiday, is counting foreign, ie out-of-state, number plates or particular kinds of vehicles such as RVs. The winner, always a child, gets some special treat at the next stop.

If the kids are keen on animals, think about a 'critter' tour. Highlights could include the **San Diego Zoo** (*page 137*), **San Diego Wild Animal Park** (*page 142*), **Aquarium of the Pacific** in Long Beach (*page 24*), the **Monterey Bay Aquarium** (*page 123*), a **whale-watching trip** or **kayaking** on Monterey Bay and the wild elk herds on **Point Reyes National Seashore** (*pages 66–67*). If the Wild West is a hot item, think **Knott's Berry Farm** (*page 27*), the ghost town of **Bodie** (*page 88*), **Columbia State Historic Park** (*page 89*) and an afternoon of **gold panning** (*page 92*) for starters.

Keeping a diary is another easy way to keep children engaged and paying attention during long drives. So is collecting, anything from admission tickets to attractions, state parks and car parks to pins and bumper stickers. And it never hurts to take a few minutes to write a postcard to friends back home. For more suggestions, check out Lonely Planet's *Travel With Children*, by Maureen Wheeler, packed with tips on how to help the whole family have a great time on the road.

After dark

California offers almost any entertainment possibility imaginable, from religious revival meetings to anonymous sex clubs, solitary communion with nature to dance clubs designed to leave you deaf, dazzled and buzzing 'til dawn.

Culture vultures can choose from world-famous symphony orchestras, opera companies, dance troupes and theatre productions as well as their less glamorous – and less pricey – counterparts. **Los Angeles** and **San Francisco** have been vying for the title of California Culture Capital for decades. San Francisco has tradition on its side – until the 1910s, Los Angeles was an economic, social and cultural backwater – but Los Angeles has the money and glamour to attract top talent. Overall, San Francisco has the edge (or at least the reputation) in opera and classical music while LA comes out ahead for dance and theatre. You're not likely to be disappointed by the top companies in either city and both attract touring artists from around the world. Both also take culture with a dose of fresh air, San Francisco with a free summer series of Sunday concerts in **Sigmund Stern Grove**, Los Angeles at the **Hollywood Bowl**.

Fortunately, there's more to the performing arts than the **San Francisco Opera**, the **Los Angeles Philharmonic**, **ACT** (American Conservatory Theater, San Francisco), the **Mark Taper Forum** (Los Angeles' leading stage), the **Old Globe Theatre** (San Diego) and similar top-tier names. Culture high and low is big business in California, where sheer numbers of people guarantee an audience for almost any type of performance. Secondary cities, places such as **San Diego** and **Sacramento**, have their own symphony orchestras and dance companies that are at least as vibrant as their larger cousins, if not as well known. Every university and college campus has an active arts programme that imports big-name performers from the far corners of the globe.

California also produces more than its share of home-grown talent, especially musicians. San Francisco and Los Angeles have been leading the musical world since the **Jefferson Airplane**, **Grateful Dead** and **The Doors** exploded onto world charts in the 1960s. The club scene in West Hollywood and San Francisco's **SOMA** reinvents itself almost by the week, but local alternative newspapers are an easy way to check on who's hot and who's not. Most clubs have an entrance fee, or cover charge; many require a minimum drink purchase, which also requires them to limit admission to those aged 21 and older.

Comedy clubs are another California first. **Robin Williams**, **Whoopie Goldberg** and **Richard Pryor** could have become stars anywhere, but it was relentless monologues and routines honed in California comedy clubs that sent their fame rocketing towards Hollywood and beyond.

everywhere. Wonder what's coming to a silver screen near you? Check local newspapers for 'sneak previews', advance screenings of about-to-be-released films that producers want to test on real audiences.

Serious cinephiles make pilgrimage to the American Cinematheque in the newly restored **Egyptian Theatre** (*6712 Hollywood Blvd, Hollywood; tel: 323-777-3456*), Hollywood's original 1922 art-deco movie palace. Two state-of-the-art cinemas have been created within

Speaking of Hollywood, California has more temples to its own adopted art form, the cinema, than the early producers who created the film capital of the world would ever have dreamed possible. Single-screen cinemas have become a rarity; multiple screen cineplexes are

the old interior, with regular programmes of avant-garde, career tributes, foreign and independent films. A documentary film, *A History of Hollywood*, plays during the day. San Francisco-area film fanatics haunt the **Pacific Film Archive** (*below the University of*

California Berkeley Art Museum, 2626 Bancroft Way, Berkeley; tel: 510-642-1412), with wildly popular showings of foreign, independent and avant-garde films. In San Francisco, the **Castro Theater** (429 Castro St; tel: 415-621-6120) shows similar fare in one of Northern California's most opulently restored cinema palaces, complete with a pipe organ which rises from the floor for concerts before and after each showing. Most college and university towns have at least one 'art theatre' specialising in similar programmes.

California has also become a haven for **film festivals**: Lake Tahoe, Los Angeles, Mill Valley, Palm Springs, San Francisco, San Jose, Santa Clarita, Sonora, Temecula and Yosemite are just a few. In fact, the state has become a haven for festivals of all kinds, in all seasons and for all reasons – or for no reason at all. Californians jump at any excuse to throw a party, from calamari (**The Great Monterey Squid Festival**, *May*) to *a cappella* music (**Vocapalooza**, *Oakland, Sept*), fog (**Pacific Coast Fog Fest**, *Pacifica, Sept*), Native Americans (**All Nations Powwow**, *Big Bear Lake, July*), pumpkins (**The Great Pumpkin Weigh-Off**, *Half Moon Bay, Oct*), lemons (**Lemon Festival**, *Goleta, Oct*), mustard (**Napa Valley Mustard Festival**, *Jan*), garlic (**Garlic Festival**, *July*) Elizabethan England (**Renaissance Faire**, *multiple locations and dates*) and more.

The single most comprehensive listing of annual festivals around the state is **California Celebrations**, an annual brochure from the California Department of Tourism. The DOT booklet **Culture's Edge** (*www.CaliforniasEdge.com*), traces the cultural fault lines that permeate Los Angeles, San Diego and San Francisco. Though intended as a cultural tour guide focusing on art and architecture, jazz and blues music, ethnic heritage (African American, Asian, Gay, Hispanic and Jewish), performances, the Gold Rush heritage and Missions, the brochure is heavy on after-dark details.

For the most current information on local events and venues, start with the local newspaper. Most daily papers have weekly entertainment sections, usually Thursday or Friday for weekend updates or Sunday for the week ahead. Traditional papers, eg the *Los Angeles Times, Sacramento Bee, San Diego Union-Tribune* and *San Francisco Chronicle*, focus on the symphony, opera, ballet, concerts and similar traditional events. Alternative papers, eg the *Los Angeles Weekly, Sacramento News & Review, San Diego Reader* and *San Francisco Bay Guardian*, devote more space to dance clubs, fringe theatre, performance art, avant-garde music and similar alternative entertainment. City magazines, slick productions devoted to life and events in their home city, also feature events calendars. Most city mags take the name of their city, eg *Los Angeles, Sacramento, San Diego*.

Don't want to wait? The **California Department of Tourism** (*www.gocalif.ca.gov*) has an annual events listing on its website. Nearly all newspapers, magazines and local convention and visitor bureaux also post events calendars on their websites. **Excite**, **Yahoo** and other web portals offer travel sections with detailed entertainment information. So does Microsoft, whose **Sidewalk** (*www.sidewalk.com*) offers detailed on-line guides to Fresno, Los Angeles, Orange County, Sacramento, San Diego, San Francisco and San Jose with up-to-the-instant entertainment information.

Getting tickets is another problem. Waiting until the last minute usually means poor seats or no seats at all.

Telephoning the box office long distance can be an exercise in expensive frustration. The easy solution is to buy tickets on-line and pick them up at show time. Most on-line ticket agencies let you search for events by location, range of dates, type of event or performer. Find the event you want, order tickets by credit card, and pick them up at the box office.

Some of the possibilities:
CultureFinder (*www.culturefinder.com*);
SportTicks (*www.sportticks.com*);
Ticket Master (*www.ticketmaster.com*);
Tix.com (*www.tix.com*);
Web Tickets (*www.webtickets.com*).

Most performance companies, bands, clubs and other venues also have their own websites with schedules and advance ticket purchase information.

Practical
information

PRACTICAL INFORMATION

Practical information

Airports

International visitors usually fly into and out of **Los Angeles International Airport** (LAX) or **San Francisco International Airport** (SFO). Both airports are under perpetual expansion; construction, confusion and delays are the norm. Luggage trolleys (carts) *may* be free in international arrivals areas, but expect to pay (US currency or credit cards) at domestic terminals. Contact individual airlines for flight information, not the airport. Larger airports have currency exchange, banking services, car-hire desks, public transport and restaurants with higher prices than quality. Smaller airports usually have cash machines (ATMs) and car-hire counters.

Currency

US dollars reign supreme in California. Banknotes can be confusing, even though the US president pictured on the front of the bill and designs on the reverse are different.

The problem: all bills, $1, $2 (rare), $5, $10, $20, $50 and $100 are the same size and printed with the same green and white colours. Banknote designs are being changed to thwart counterfeiting, so you may see two different versions of $100, $50 and $20 bills.

Each dollar has 100 cents; coins are: the penny (1 cent), nickel (5 cents), dime (10 cents), quarter (25 cents), half dollar (50 cents, rare) and silver dollar ($1, seldom seen outside Nevada casinos).

Climate

California's patchwork terrain creates a confounding patchwork of microclimates and weather patterns. Expect sunshine in Southern California, fog along the coast, and heat inland. Coastal fog is common in summer, especially in Northern California. Grey skies can hang low all day or go brilliant blue beneath a blistering sun. In winter, temperatures drop with altitude and distance north. Expect snow above 1500m. In summer, expect increasing heat inland, with 113°F (45°C) plus in the deserts.

Banks can exchange foreign currency and non-US dollar traveller's cheques, but expect delays outside airport and big-city tourist area banks. US dollar traveller's cheques from well-known issuers such as Thomas Cook are acceptable everywhere. To report lost or stolen Thomas Cook Travellers Cheques: *tel: 800-223-7373*.

You can also get cash from automated teller machines, ATMs, either by cash withdrawal or credit card advance. The most common networks are **Star** and **Cirrus**. Both require a four-digit PIN (personal identification number), which must be assigned before you leave home.

Carry at least one (preferably two) major credit card such as **Access** (known as **MasterCard** in the US), **American Express**, or **Visa**. Car-hire agencies, hotels, motels and most other businesses which require a deposit demand either a credit card or a large cash deposit, even if the bill has been pre-paid or will eventually be paid by cash.

Customs regulations

US duty-free limits apply to all visitors: 1 litre of spirits or wine, 120 cigarettes and 100 cigars (so long as they aren't from Cuba) and up to $100-worth of gifts. The age limit is 18 for tobacco and 21 for alcohol.

Check with your own customs officials for duty-free allowances going home, but skip the heavily advertised 'duty free' shops. Alcohol, perfume, tobacco and anything else you might want to take home are cheaper at supermarkets and discount stores than at airport and downtown duty-free stores.

Disabled travellers

State and federal laws require all business or services that deal with the public – hotels, cinemas, museums, post offices and the like – to be accessible to handicapped people. Most city streets have kerb ramps at intersections. Major parks have occasional sealed pathways for disabled visitors.

SATH (Society for the Advancement of Travel for the Handicapped) (*347 5th Ave, Suite 610, New York NY 10016; tel: 212-447-7284*), has specific information. The annual *Holidays and Travel Abroad* brochure produced by

RADAR (*12 City Forum, 250 City Rd, London EC1V 8AF; tel: (0171) 250 3222*) details facilities for the disabled in several countries, including the US.

Drinking

The drinking age, 21, is strictly enforced. Alcohol may be sold between 0600 and 0200. Beer, wine and spirits are on offer in food, drug and convenience stores as well as liquor stores, but individual drinks cannot be taken out from bars and pubs.

Anyone stopped by the police for apparent drunk driving, usually called DUI (driving under the influence), can choose between a blood, breath or urine test for alcohol. Refusing to test is a *de facto* admission of guilt. Heavy fines, jail sentences and suspension of driving privileges are the usual punishments for DUI.

Electricity

All electrical power is 110 volt, 60 Hertz. Power points require plugs with two flat, parallel prongs. Some big-city hotels have adapters, but it's easier to bring your own or buy them from Radio Shack or some similar electronics supply shop.

Entry formalities

Visitors to the US generally need a passport, visa and proof of return travel. Citizens of some countries can obtain tourist visas upon entry, but most travellers must obtain visas before arriving in the US. Check with the nearest US consulate or embassy for current requirements at least three months before travel. Weapons and narcotics may not be imported – carry a doctor's prescription to prove that any medication is legitimate.

Health

For immediate help in life-threatening situations, dial 911, a free call from any telephone. When a life is at stake, care comes first, payment a distant second.

For more mundane health problems, most hospitals maintain 24-hour emergency rooms for walk-in care. Be prepared to pay on the spot, either by cash or credit card. For sneezes, sniffles and other minor complaints,

you can sometimes get informal advice from a pharmacist, but only a genuine physician can provide medical care.

US medical providers almost *never* accept non-US medical insurance or other health plan coverage. Most travel agencies which sell international travel also sell short-term health insurance to cover costs incurred in the US – with US hospital costs topping well over $1000 per day, insurance is a good idea.

Any traveller taking prescription medication should bring enough for the entire trip, plus a few days extra in case of delay. Since drug names are different in different countries, bring a copy of your prescription that shows the generic (chemical) name and formulation of your drug, not just the brand name.

No inoculations are required for travel to California. This is a reasonably healthy place, but never drink water that doesn't come from the tap or a bottle – ground water is contaminated with *giardia* and other parasites. Sunglasses, broad-brimmed hats and sunscreen help prevent sunburn and heat-related problems. Be sure to drink plenty of water and other non-alcoholic liquids, especially in hot weather.

Information sources

For general information, contact the California Division of Tourism (*801 K St, Ste 1600, Sacramento CA 95814; tel: 916-322-2881 or 800-863-2543; web: http://www.gocalif.ca.gov*).

For national park, monument and seashore information, contact National Parks of the West (*Western Region Information Center,*

SAN FRANCISCO

SAN FRANCISCO
DOWNTOWN

Fort Mason, Bldg 201, San Francisco CA 94125; tel: 415-556-0560; web: http://www.nps.gov).

For **California** state parks and beaches, contact **State of California Department of Parks and Recreation** (*PO Box 942896, Sacramento CA 94926; tel: 916-653-6995 or 800-444-7275; web: http://www.cal-parks.ca.gov*). For state park camping reservations, contact **ParkNet** (*PO Box 1510, Rancho Cordova, CA 95741; tel: 800-444-7275*).

Insurance

Travel insurance should cover your holiday investment, your health and possibly your belongings. Trip cancellation and delay cover will take care of any additional expenses if flights are cancelled or delayed, or if you must cancel due to illness or similar emergency. It's also wise to buy cover for medical expenses and evacuation in case of severe injury or illness.

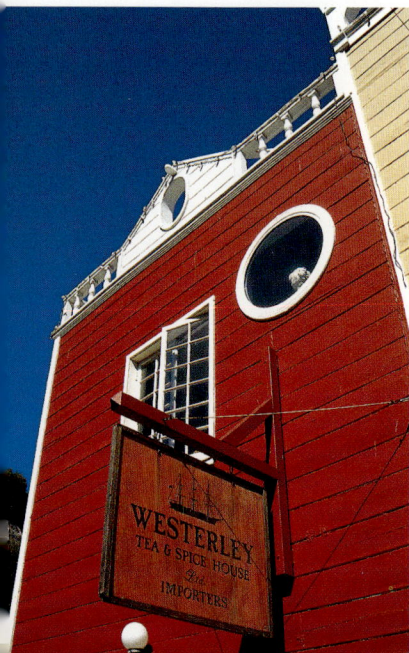

Maps

The most generally useful road maps come from the **American Automobile Association (AAA)**, free to AAA members. AAA maps, books and other travel products are distributed in Northern California by the **California State Automobile Association** and in Southern California by the **Automobile Association of Southern California**. Ask your own auto club about reciprocal agreements with the AAA. If a service is free at home, it's free at AAA when you show your membership card.

On the commercial side, **Rand McNally** produce good large-scale maps; **Thomas Brothers** sell books of highly detailed maps.

Opening times

Americans are workaholics. Most offices are open Mon–Fri 0900–1700; many tourist offices are open weekends as well. Banks generally open Mon–Thur 1000–1600, Fri 0900–1800 and Sat 0900–1300. ATMs operate 24 hours.

Expect shopping malls to open by 1000 and close 2000–2200, earlier Sat and Sun. Restaurants, theatres and museums often close Mon, but cinemas and most tourist attractions stay open all week.

Public holidays

1 Jan New Year's Day
3rd Mon in Jan Martin Luther King Day
12 Feb Lincoln's Birthday
3rd Mon in Feb President's Day
Sun in Mar/Apr Easter Day
Last Mon in May Memorial Day
4 July Independence Day
1st Mon in Sept Labor Day
9 Sept California Admission Day
2nd Mon in Oct Columbus Day
11 Nov Veterans Day
4th Thur in Nov Thanksgiving Day
25 Dec Christmas Day

Unofficial holidays such as the lunar Chinese New Year (Jan/Feb), St Patrick's Day (17 Mar) and Cinco de Mayo (5 May, Mexican Independence from Spain) get as much attention as official holidays in ethnic and non-ethnic areas alike.

Tourist attractions generally remain open on official holidays. Post offices and government offices close and department stores stage huge holiday sales. Almost all establishments close for Thanksgiving and Christmas, both major family days.

Reading

AAA sell excellent regional guides by the Automobile Club of Southern California: *Desert Area; Central Coast* (Ventura, Santa Barbara and San Luis Obispo Counties); and S*an Diego County*.

The Adventurer's Guide to the Sierra Nevada Mountains, by Claire and Marty Hiester (1995, design Works!, Incline Village, NV).

Adventuring in the California Desert, by Lynne Foster (1998, Sierra Club Books, San Francisco).

Big Sur and the Oranges of Hieronymus Bosch, by Henry Miller (1957, New Directions Publishing Company, New York).

California Historical Landmarks (1990, Office of Historic Preservation, California Department of Parks and Recreation).

California Wildlife Viewing Guide, by Jeanne Clark (1989, Falcon Press, Helena, MT).

The Electric Kool-Aid Acid Test, by Tom Wolfe (1983, Bantam Books, New York).

The Grapes of Wrath, by John Steinbeck (multiple editions).

Humbugs and Heroes, by Richard Dillon (1983, Yosemite-DiMaggio, Oakland, CA).

The Joy Luck Club, by Amy Tan (1994, Ivy Books, New York).

The Kitchen God's Wife, by Amy Tan (1992, Ivy Books, New York).

L.A. Bizarro, by Anthony Lovett and Matt Maranian (1997, St Martin's Press, New York).

The L.A. Musical History Tour, by Art Fein (1998, 2.13.61 Publications, Los Angeles).

The Literary Hills of San Francisco, by Luree Miller (1992, Starrhill Press, Washington, DC).

Los Angeles The Rich Bastards Guide, by Simon St Goar Kelton (1998, RBG Publishing, Los Angeles).

The Mountains of California, by John Muir (1997, Penguin USA, New York).

My First Summer in the Sierra, by John Muir (1998, Chapters Publishing Ltd).

Napa, by James Conaway (1990, Avon Books, New York).

COME BACK
IN TIME
TO THE
CANNERY
ROW
of JOHN STEINBECK'S

SPIRIT of MONTEREY

WAX MUSEUM

JOURNEY INTO THE PAST
— from the —
SPANISH DISCOVERY
— to —
JOHN STEINBECK
A 30 MINUTE VOYAGE

On the Road Around California, by Fred Gebhart and Maxine Cass (1997, Thomas Cook Publishing, London).

Outdoor Getaway Guide, Northern California, by Tom Stienstra (1998, Foghorn Press, Petaluma, CA).

The Painted Ladies Guide to Victorian California, by Elizabeth Pomada and Michael Larsen (1991, Dutton Studio Books, New York).

Permanent Californians, by Judi Culbertson and Tom Randall (1989, Chelsea Green Publishing Company, Chelsea, VT).

Roughing It, by Mark Twain (multiple editions).

San Francisco The Musical History Tour, by Joel Selvin (1996, Chronicle Books, San Francisco).

Tales of the City, by Armistead Maupin (1994, Harperennial Library, New York).

Two Years Before the Mast, Richard Henry Dana (multiple editions).

The Ultimate Hollywood Tour Book, by William A Gordon (1998, North Ridge Books, El Toro, CA).

Unknown California, ed by Jonathan Eisen, David Fine with Kim Eisen (1985, Collier Books, New York).

Weekend Adventures in Northern California, by Carole Terwilliger Meyers (1997, Carousel Press, Berkeley, CA).

Safety and security

Dial **911**, a free call from any telephone, for quick emergency help from police, fire, medical or other authorities.

Use the same common-sense precautions you'd use in any big city: don't flash your cash; walk as though you know where you're going; don't wander down dark alley-ways; avoid neighbourhoods filled with barbed wire, barred windows and similar signs of danger.

Smoking

Tobacco is legal in California, but smoking isn't in most indoor places. It's usually safe to smoke out of doors in urban areas, but not in bars, restaurants, theatres, offices, aeroplanes, buses and other enclosed spaces. Smoking is often banned along trails in summer when the fire danger is extreme.

Telephones

Look for the familiar sign with a white telephone on a blue field. Dialling instructions are usually posted on public (pay) telephones. Local calls generally cost 35 cents. Toll-free calls, ie, calls to area codes 800, 877 and 888, are free. So are 911 emergency calls.

To locate local phone numbers, dial 411. For long-distance information, dial 1 + area code + 555-1212. For international enquiries, dial 00. Information calls are never free; the cost depends on the telephone company which operates the telephone.

Hotels and motels often add heavy surcharges to the cost of calls made from rooms, but there are no surcharges for the pay phones in the lobby. To save money, buy a pre-paid telephone card from any post office, newsagent, drug store, supermarket, tourist office or other vendor. Phone cards purchased outside the US are seldom accepted.

To place an international call, dial 011 (access code) + country code + city code (drop the first zero if there is one) + local number. To call inner London, for example, dial 011-44-171 + local number.

Time

California is in the Pacific Time Zone. Pacific Standard Time, PST, is GMT minus 8 hours. Pacific Daylight Time, PDT (first Sun in Apr to last Sun in Oct), is GST minus 7 hours.

Tipping

Very few California restaurants or hotels add a service charge, but almost all waiters/waitresses and other servers depend heavily on tips for the bulk of their income. A 15 per cent tip is standard, 20 per cent is expected in more expensive restaurants. It's also allowed to leave two pennies if the service is especially poor. Hotel porters get $1 per bag, valet parking attendants $1–$5, bartenders $1 per drink and taxi drivers 15 per cent of the meter fare.

Toilets

The American euphemisms are **restroom** or **bathroom**, though the Canadian **washroom** is generally understood. 'Loo' or 'WC' will probably get blank stares. The usual designations are 'Men' and 'Women', increasingly indicated with male and female figures. You may see *caballeros* or *señors* (male) and *damas* (female) in Spanish-speaking areas and Hispanic restaurants. Ultra-chic bars and remote recreation areas often have unisex toilets.

Index

Editorial, design and production credits

Project management: Dial House Publishing Services

Series editor: Christopher Catling

Copy editor: Posy Gosling

Proof-reader: Susie Whimster

Series and cover design: Trickett & Webb Limited

Cover artwork: Wenham Arts

Text layout: Wenham Arts

Map work: RJS Associates

Repro and image setting: Z2 Repro, Thetford, Norfolk, UK

Printed and bound by: Artes Graficas ELKAR S. Coop., Bilbao, Spain

We would like to thank the authors for the photographs used in this book, to whom the copyright in the photographs belong.